Better Homes and Gardens®
DESSERTS

BETTER HOMES AND GARDENS® BOOKS

Editor Gerald M. Knox
Art Director Ernest Shelton
Managing Editor David A. Kirchner
Copy and Production Editors James D. Blume, Marsha Jahns, Rosanne Weber Mattson, Mary Helen Schiltz

Food and Nutrition Editor Nancy Byal
Department Head, Cook Books Sharyl Heiken
Associate Department Heads Sandra Granseth, Rosemary C. Hutchinson, Elizabeth Woolever
Senior Food Editors Julia Malloy, Marcia Stanley, Joyce Trollope
Associate Food Editors Linda Henry, Mary Major, Diana McMillen, Mary Jo Plutt, Maureen Powers, Martha Schiel, Linda Foley Woodrum
Recipe Development Editor Marion Viall
Test Kitchen Director Sharon Stilwell
Test Kitchen Photo Studio Director Janet Pittman
Test Kitchen Home Economists Lynn Blanchard, Jean Brekke, Kay Cargill, Marilyn Cornelius, Jennifer Darling, Maryellyn Krantz, Lynelle Munn, Dianna Nolin, Marge Steenson

Associate Art Directors Linda Ford Vermie, Neoma Alt West, Randall Yontz
Assistant Art Directors Lynda Haupert, Harijs Priekulis, Tom Wegner
Senior Graphic Designers Jack Murphy, Stan Sams, Darla Whipple-Frain
Graphic Designers Mike Burns, Sally Cooper, Blake Welch, Brian Wignall, Kimberly Zarley

Vice President, Editorial Director Doris Eby
Executive Director, Editorial Services Duane L. Gregg

President, Book Group Fred Stines
Director of Publishing Robert B. Nelson
Vice President, Retail Marketing Jamie Martin
Vice President, Direct Marketing Arthur Heydendael

Desserts
Editor Joyce Trollope
Copy and Production Editor Rosanne Weber Mattson
Graphic Designer Lynda Haupert
Electronic Text Processor Donna Russell
Photographers Michael Jensen and Sean Fitzgerald
Food Stylists Suzanne Finley, Dianna Nolin, Janet Pittman, Maria Rolandelli

On the cover
Easy Vanilla Ice Cream, Chocolate Ice Cream, and Strawberry Ice Cream (see recipes, page 38).

Our seal assures you that every recipe in *Desserts* has been tested in the Better Homes and Gardens® Test Kitchen. This means that each recipe is practical and reliable, and meets our high standards of taste appeal.

Is a rich, homemade dessert your idea of paradise? Then you've come to the right place! Sweet dreams are made of the recipes found within the covers of *Desserts*.

Here's a savory spectrum of delights to satisfy all tastes. Try dazzling desserts such as meringues or phyllo diamonds that fit the most elegant occasion. Or, choose from such comforting favorites as fruit crisps and fresh-from-the-oven pies. There are even slimmed-down recipe selections that boast a low calorie count.

So, go ahead. Let visions of sugar plums dance through your head as you page through this dessert-lover's dream book. The mouthwatering photographs and clear-cut instructions make the recipes all the more irresistible.

Contents

Introduction
3

Simmered Compotes
6

Simple, satisfying, and slimming—our fruit desserts have it all. Serve them plain or capped with a sauce.

Flavorful Fruit Crisps
10

Succulent fruit and a crisp topping bake together for a cherished, old-fashioned dessert favorite.

Treats from the Cookie Jar
14

Everything from drop cookies to bars . . . enough to keep your cookie jar full.

Stack a Shortcake
42

Here you'll find a combination of shortcake, fresh fruit, and whipping cream, renowned for their power to please.

Creamy Puddings
48

Serve our smooth and creamy puddings plain and simple or gussied up for company.

Chilly Sherbets And Ices
54

Cool your palate with a refreshing treat. Try a big scoop or two for a true culinary delicacy.

Spectacular Meringues
60

Transform a plain, simple egg into elegant meringues. They're light as a cloud and melt in your mouth.

Piecrust Creations
90

Sit yourself down to a wedge of home-baked pie. There's nothing like it— flaky pastry and luscious pie filling!

Choice Cream Puffs
96

A handsome dessert to fill and decorate as you please.

Flaky Phyllo Diamonds
102

The tastiest, flakiest creation you'll ever put together. The secret: Just start with purchased phyllo dough.

Magnificent Baked Soufflés
106

Delicately light, a very impressive dessert to serve for special friends.

Bountiful Baked Fruit
20

Apples and pears—perfect fruits for you to fill and bake for an uncommonly delicious treat.

Old-Fashioned Cobblers
24

A fluffy, sweet biscuit covers the flavor-packed fruit filling in these time-honored favorites.

Bake a Cake
30

These recipes are·worth the time it takes to bake a cake from scratch. Here we've given a new twist to some old favorites.

Homemade Ice Creams
36

Whether you lick your ice cream from a cone or a spoon, you'll love our collection of flavors.

Class-Act Custards
66

Turn staples—eggs, milk, and sugar—into delightful, people-pleasing sweets.

Luscious Cheesecakes
72

Indulge! Bake an exquisite cheesecake for an outstanding after-dinner taste treat.

Shapely Crepes
80

Crepes please the palate and delight the eye. Have some fun and make crepes for dessert.

Puff Pastry Panache
86

A spectacular-looking dessert that begins with purchased frozen puff pastry. You'll love the delicious results.

Show-Off Gelatin Desserts
112

Make-ahead specialties for an easy, yet classy final course.

Dinner Finalés
120

Special Helps
Simple endings for special meals.

Nutrition Analysis Chart
122

Index
125

Simmered Compotes

What's easy to fix, low in calories, and good to eat? You'll find the answer right here, in our delicious fruit-filled compotes.

The lightly sweetened syrups turn tasty fruit combinations into delightfully satisfying desserts. And each compote serving boasts fewer calories than a carton of flavored yogurt!

Poached Nectarines and Grapes

Poached Nectarines And Grapes

A fresh fruit fix-up with just 134 calories a serving.

1 **orange**
¾ **cup water**
⅓ **cup sugar**
2 **teaspoons vanilla**
3 **nectarines, pitted and quartered**
¾ **cup seedless red *or* green grapes, halved**

Remove a 2x1-inch strip of peel from the orange (see photo 1). Save the rest of the orange to use in another recipe. For the syrup, in a medium saucepan stir together water, sugar, and vanilla (see photo 2). Add orange peel strip. Bring to boiling, stirring till sugar is dissolved. Add nectarines to syrup in saucepan. Bring to boiling. Reduce heat, then simmer, covered, about 5 minutes or till fruit is just tender. Remove the saucepan from heat.

Transfer nectarines and syrup to a bowl. Remove orange peel and stir in grapes. Cool slightly. Serve warm or chill, covered, several hours or overnight. Serve in dessert dishes (see photo 3). If desired, garnish with fresh mint sprigs. Makes 4 servings.

Microwave Directions: In a 1½-quart non-metal casserole stir together water, sugar, and vanilla. Add orange peel. Micro-cook, uncovered, on 100% power (HIGH) about 2 minutes or till sugar is dissolved; stir after 1 minute. Add nectarines. Micro-cook, covered, on 100% power (HIGH) about 3 minutes more or till fruit is just tender. Remove orange peel and stir in grapes. Cool slightly. Serve as above.

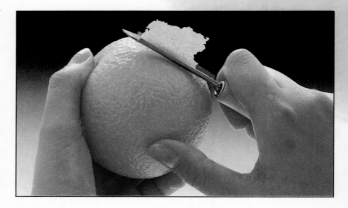

1 Use a vegetable peeler or small sharp knife to easily remove a thin strip of orange peel. Leave the bitter white membrane attached to the orange flesh, not to the peel.

2 In a 2-quart saucepan stir together the ingredients for the syrup. Although the saucepan may seem too large for the syrup, you'll need the extra space to stir in the fruit.

Gingery Apricot-Banana Compote

1	17-ounce can unpeeled apricot halves
¾	cup orange juice
1	tablespoon finely chopped crystallized ginger
1	medium banana
¼	cup toasted coconut

Drain apricots, reserving ½ cup syrup. For syrup, in a medium saucepan combine reserved syrup, orange juice, and crystallized ginger (see photo 2). Bring to boiling. Reduce heat, then simmer, uncovered, for 5 minutes. Stir in apricots. Bring to boiling. Reduce heat, then simmer, uncovered, for 3 minutes. Remove the saucepan from heat.

Transfer fruit and syrup to a bowl. Cool slightly. Serve warm or chill, covered, several hours or overnight. Bias-slice banana; gently stir banana into apricot mixture. Serve in dessert dishes (see photo 3). Sprinkle coconut atop. Serves 5.

Microwave Directions: Drain apricots, reserving ½ cup syrup. In a 1½-quart nonmetal casserole stir together reserved syrup, orange juice, and ginger. Micro-cook, uncovered, on 100% power (HIGH) for 2 to 3 minutes or till mixture is boiling. Micro-cook on 100% power (HIGH) for 1 minute more. Stir in apricots. Micro-cook, uncovered, on 100% power (HIGH) about 3 minutes or till bubbly around edges; stir after 1 minute. Cool slightly. Serve as above.

3 To simplify serving, first spoon out equal portions of the fruit pieces into the dessert dishes. Then pour the syrup into each dish, dividing it evenly.

Flavorful Fruit Crisps

Contrasting food textures, such as soft and crunchy or smooth and bumpy, add to eating enjoyment.

Our simple fruit crisps give you some pleasurable contrasting textures. The cooked fruit is tender and the topping is crisp.

Make either of our dessert crisps and give your tongue a real taste thrill.

Caramel Pear-Peach Crisp

Caramel Pear-Peach Crisp

½ cup quick-cooking rolled oats
¼ cup packed brown sugar
¼ cup whole bran cereal
3 tablespoons whole wheat flour
¾ teaspoon pumpkin pie spice *or* ground cinnamon
¼ cup butter *or* margarine
4 to 5 medium pears
2 medium peaches
⅓ cup caramel ice cream topping
Vanilla ice cream

In a mixing bowl stir together oats, sugar, bran cereal, flour, and pie spice or cinnamon. Cut in butter or margarine till the mixture resembles coarse crumbs (see photo 1). Set aside.

Peel, core, and slice pears (see photo 2). Peel, remove pits, and slice peaches. Measure 5 cups sliced fruit. Transfer fruit to a 10x6x2-inch baking dish, spreading in an even layer. Drizzle caramel topping over fruit. Sprinkle oat mixture over fruit (see photo 3).

Bake, uncovered, in a 350° oven for 30 to 35 minutes or till fruit is tender when tested with a fork and oat topping is lightly browned. Serve warm with ice cream. Makes 6 servings.

1 For the crumb mixture, use a pastry blender to cut the butter into the dry ingredients. Between strokes, remove any butter that sticks to the pastry blender with a rubber spatula. Cut in till the pieces are the size of coarse crumbs.

2 A quick way to peel the pears is to cut them lengthwise into halves, then into quarters. Working with one wedge at a time, cut peel from each piece, removing as little fruit as possible. Then, remove the core from each wedge. Cut the wedges into ¼- to ½-inch-thick slices.

Apple-Granola Crisp

Choose firm apples for baking, such as Rome Beauty and Granny Smith.

2	**tablespoons butter *or* margarine**
⅓	**cup finely crushed graham crackers**
⅓	**cup granola, crushed**
7	**medium cooking apples**
1	**tablespoon brown sugar**
½	**cup apple juice *or* cider**

In a mixing bowl cut butter or margarine into graham crackers till mixture resembles coarse crumbs (*see* photo 1). Stir in granola. Set aside.

Peel, core, and slice apples (*see* photo 2). Measure 6 cups sliced fruit. Toss fruit with sugar. Transfer fruit mixture to a 10x6x2-inch baking dish. Pour apple juice over fruit mixture. Sprinkle crumb mixture over fruit (*see* photo 3).

Bake, uncovered, in a 350° oven for 35 to 40 minutes or till fruit is tender when tested with a fork. Serve warm. Makes 6 servings.

Peach-Granola Crisp: Prepare Apple-Granola Crisp as above, *except* omit apples and use 9 medium *peaches;* reduce apple juice to 2 *tablespoons.* Peel, remove pits, and slice peaches. Measure 6 cups sliced fruit. Toss fruit with sugar. Transfer fruit mixture to a 10x6x2-inch baking dish. Drizzle apple juice over fruit mixture. Sprinkle crumb mixture over fruit. Bake, uncovered, in a 350° oven for 30 to 35 minutes or till fruit is tender. Serve warm.

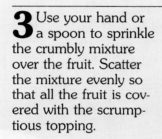

3 Use your hand or a spoon to sprinkle the crumbly mixture over the fruit. Scatter the mixture evenly so that all the fruit is covered with the scrumptious topping.

Treats from the Cookie Jar

According to an old saying, "Variety is the spice of life." To help spice up your life, we've gathered a variety of cookie flavors in this chapter.

Keep your cookie jar stocked with any of these treats—from freely shaped drops to perfectly cut bars. They're all so delicious that you're bound to grab for just one more.

Banana-Orange Soft Drops

Banana-Orange Soft Drops

1	cup all-purpose flour
¾	teaspoon baking powder
⅛	teaspoon baking soda
⅛	teaspoon salt
¼	cup butter *or* margarine
½	cup sugar
1	egg
1½	teaspoons finely shredded orange peel
⅓	cup mashed ripe banana (1 medium)
2	tablespoons orange juice
	Butter Frosting
	Finely chopped pecans (optional)

1 Stir together the dry ingredients in a bowl. Mixing the dry ingredients together ensures that the leavening and salt are well distributed throughout the flour before it's added to the creamed mixture.

Stir together flour, baking powder, baking soda, and salt (see photo 1). In a small mixer bowl beat butter or margarine with an electric mixer on medium speed for 30 seconds. Add sugar and beat till fluffy (see photo 2). Add egg and orange peel; beat well. Combine banana and orange juice. Add flour mixture and banana mixture alternately to beaten mixture and beat till well mixed (see photo 3).

Drop by level tablespoons 2 inches apart onto a lightly greased cookie sheet (see photo 4). Bake in a 350° oven about 10 minutes or till cookies are set and edges are lightly browned. Cool 1 minute before removing from cookie sheet; cool on a wire rack (see photo 5). When cool, frost with Butter Frosting. Sprinkle with nuts, if desired. Makes about 30 cookies.

Butter Frosting: In a small mixer bowl beat 2 tablespoons *butter or margarine* with an electric mixer on medium speed till softened. Gradually add ⅔ cup sifted *powdered sugar,* beating well. Beat in 2 teaspoons *milk* and ½ teaspoon *vanilla.* Gradually beat in ⅔ cup sifted *powdered sugar.* Beat in enough *milk* (about 1 teaspoon) to make frosting spreadable.

2 Soften the butter by beating it with an electric mixer until creamy. Then add the sugar and beat until the mixture is fluffy. Occasionally scrape the sides of the bowl with a rubber spatula so the dough is evenly mixed.

3 To alternately add liquid and dry ingredients, spoon about a third of the dry ingredients into the creamed mixture; beat thoroughly. Then add half of the liquid. Next comes another third of the dry ingredients, then the remaining liquid ingredients, and finally the remaining dry ingredients. Beat after each addition so that the mixture is evenly moistened.

4 Drop the dough onto a cookie sheet. Use a rubber spatula or another spoon to push the dough off of the spoon. By dropping the dough 2 inches apart, you allow for spreading as the cookies bake.

When a recipe calls for a level tablespoon, use a measuring spoon. For rounded tea-spoons, use a flatware spoon.

5 Use a pancake turner or a wide metal spatula to transfer the cookies from the cookie sheet to a wire cooling rack. The rack allows air to circulate around the cookies.

Stack the cookies only after they are completely cool.

Coconut-Oatmeal Cookies

½ **cup all-purpose flour**
½ **teaspoon baking soda**
½ **cup shortening**
¼ **cup butter *or* margarine**
½ **cup sugar**
½ **cup packed brown sugar**
1 **egg**
1 **teaspoon vanilla**
2 **cups quick-cooking rolled oats**
1 **cup coconut**

Stir together flour, baking soda, and ¼ teaspoon *salt* (see photo 1, page 16). In a small mixer bowl beat shortening and butter or margarine with an electric mixer on medium speed for 30 seconds. Add sugar and brown sugar and beat till fluffy (see photo 2, page 16). Add egg and vanilla; beat well. Add flour mixture, then beat till well mixed. Stir in oats and coconut.

Drop by rounded teaspoons 2 inches apart onto an ungreased cookie sheet (see photo 4, page 17). Bake in a 375° oven for 9 to 11 minutes or till tops are golden. Remove; cool on a wire rack (see photo 5, page 17). Makes about 48.

Peanut Butter Drops

1 **cup all-purpose flour**
½ **cup finely crushed graham crackers**
1 **teaspoon baking powder**
½ **cup peanut butter**
¼ **cup butter *or* margarine**
¾ **cup packed brown sugar**
2 **eggs**
1 **teaspoon vanilla**
1 **cup candy-coated milk chocolate pieces, candy-coated peanut butter-flavored pieces, *or* semisweet chocolate pieces**

Stir together flour, graham crackers, and baking powder (see photo 1, page 16). In a small mixer bowl beat peanut butter and butter or margarine with an electric mixer on medium speed for 30 seconds. Add brown sugar and beat till fluffy

(see photo 2, page 16). Add eggs and vanilla; beat well. Add flour mixture then beat till well mixed. Stir in chocolate or peanut butter pieces. Drop by rounded teaspoons 2 inches apart onto an ungreased cookie sheet (see photo 4, page 17). Bake in a 350° oven for 10 to 12 minutes or till edges are brown. Remove and cool on a wire rack (see photo 5, page 17). Makes 36.

Double-Chocolate Pudding Drops

Top the cookies with chocolate frosting and nuts, or leave them unadorned. Scrumptious either way!

1¼ **cups all-purpose flour**
½ **teaspoon baking soda**
½ **cup shortening**
1 **4-serving-size package *instant* chocolate pudding mix**
¼ **cup packed brown sugar**
1 **egg**
1 **teaspoon vanilla**
¼ **cup milk**
1 **6-ounce package (1 cup) semisweet chocolate pieces**

Stir together flour, baking soda, and ¼ teaspoon *salt* (see photo 1, page 16). In a small mixer bowl beat shortening with an electric mixer on medium speed for 30 seconds. Add dry pudding mix and brown sugar and beat till fluffy (see photo 2, page 16). Add egg and vanilla; beat well. Add flour mixture and milk alternately to beaten mixture and beat till well mixed (see photo 3, page 16). Stir in chocolate pieces.

Drop by rounded teaspoons 2 inches apart onto an ungreased cookie sheet (see photo 4, page 17). Bake in a 350° oven for 10 to 12 minutes or till cookies are set. Remove and cool on a wire rack (see photo 5, page 17). If desired, frost with canned chocolate frosting; sprinkle with chopped nuts. Makes about 36.

Spicy Date Drop Cookies

Well-suited for holiday baking, but great any time.

¾ cup all-purpose flour
¾ cup whole wheat flour
½ teaspoon baking powder
½ teaspoon baking soda
½ teaspoon ground nutmeg
½ teaspoon ground cinnamon
¼ teaspoon salt
½ cup shortening
¾ cup packed brown sugar
1 egg
1 teaspoon vanilla
⅓ cup milk
1½ cups bran flakes
1 cup pitted whole dates, snipped
½ cup chopped walnuts

Stir together all-purpose flour, whole wheat flour, baking powder, baking soda, nutmeg, cinnamon, and salt (see photo 1, page 16).

In a small mixer bowl beat shortening with an electric mixer on medium speed for 30 seconds. Add brown sugar and beat till fluffy (see photo 2, page 16). Add egg and vanilla; beat well. Add flour mixture and milk alternately to beaten mixture and beat till well mixed (see photo 3, page 16). Stir in cereal, dates, and nuts.

Drop by rounded teaspoons 2 inches apart onto an ungreased cookie sheet (see photo 4, page 17). Bake in a 350° oven for 9 to 11 minutes or till lightly browned on bottom. Remove and cool on a wire rack (see photo 5, page 17). Makes about 60 cookies.

Carrot-Orange Bars

Shredded carrots give these frosted cake bar cookies their orange color.

1 cup all-purpose flour
½ teaspoon baking powder
¼ teaspoon baking soda
¼ teaspoon salt
¼ cup butter *or* margarine
½ cup sugar
1 egg
1 teaspoon vanilla
½ teaspoon finely shredded orange peel
½ cup milk
1½ cups finely shredded carrots
   (3 medium carrots)
Cream Cheese Frosting

Grease an 11x7x1½-inch baking pan. Stir together flour, baking powder, baking soda, and salt (see photo 1, page 16).

In a small mixer bowl beat butter or margarine with an electric mixer on medium speed for 30 seconds. Add sugar and beat till fluffy (see photo 2, page 16). Add egg, vanilla, and orange peel; beat well. Add flour mixture and milk alternately to beaten mixture and beat till well mixed (see photo 3, page 16). Stir in carrots.

Spread batter in the prepared pan. Bake in a 350° oven about 25 minutes or till a wooden toothpick inserted near center comes out clean. Cool on a wire rack. Frost with Cream Cheese Frosting. Cut into bars. Store in the refrigerator. Makes 24 bars.

Cream Cheese Frosting: In a small mixer bowl soften one 3-ounce package *cream cheese.* Add 1¼ cups sifted *powdered sugar* and ¼ teaspoon *vanilla;* beat till fluffy. If necessary, beat in enough *milk* (about 1 teaspoon) to make frosting spreadable. Makes about ⅔ cup.

Bountiful Baked Fruit

What do apples and pears have in common? They're perfectly shaped for stuffing and baking.

The stuffing steps are a breeze. Just hollow out the core and load the fruit with a quick filling. Next, pop the fruit into the oven to simmer in a tasty sauce.

Serve the fruit in a bowl for an uncommonly good-tasting fruit dessert.

Orange-Sauced Baked Apples

Orange-Sauced Baked Apples

6	**medium cooking apples (about 2 pounds)**
¼	**cup pitted whole dates, snipped**
2	**tablespoons chopped walnuts**
1½	**cups orange juice**
1	**4-serving-size package *instant* vanilla pudding mix**
2	**tablespoons light corn syrup**
1	**tablespoon lemon juice**

Peel apples and remove cores (see photo 1). Enlarge openings slightly (see photo 2). If desired, score apples with the tines of a fork (see photo 3).

Place apples in a 3-quart casserole. Combine dates and walnuts. Fill centers of apples with date-nut mixture (see photo 4).

For sauce, in a small mixing bowl stir orange juice into the dry pudding mix. Stir in corn syrup and lemon juice. Pour mixture over apples, coating each well. Bake, covered, in a 350° oven about 40 minutes or till apples are just tender, basting once with sauce (see photo 5). Let cool, uncovered, about 30 minutes. To serve, place apples in dessert dishes; stir sauce and spoon over apples. Serve warm. Makes 6 servings.

Microwave Directions: Prepare apples and filling as above. Place apples in a nonmetal 3-quart casserole. Fill with date-nut mixture. Prepare the sauce; pour over apples. Micro-cook, covered, on 100% power (HIGH) for 9 to 11 minutes or till apples are just tender, giving dish a quarter-turn, rotating apples, and basting with sauce twice. Let stand, then serve as above.

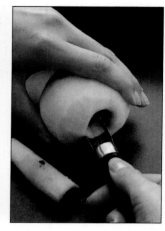

1 To remove core, use a fruit corer or a sharp knife. On cutting board, press corer into peeled fruit starting at the stem end. Aim for the blossom end and remove the core down the center. Pick up fruit and remove core as shown.

2 Use the fruit corer or a small knife to cut the hole slightly larger. This makes room for more filling in the center of the fruit.

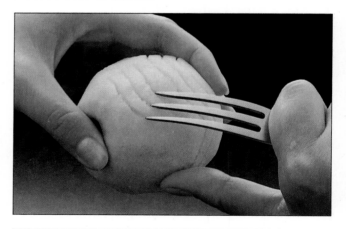

3 To make the attractive pattern on the outside of the apple, using the tines of a fork score the fruit. Start at the top of the apple and work in a circular pattern around the apple until you reach the base of the fruit.

Elegant Baked Pears

Stick with your diet even though you're entertaining. This sophisticated pear dessert keeps the calories right around 200 for a serving.

4 **fresh pears**
2 **tablespoons apricot preserves, cut up**
2 **tablespoons sliced almonds,**
  toasted and chopped
½ **cup dry white wine**
2 **tablespoons crème de cassis**
1 **tablespoon sugar**
½ **teaspoon finely shredded lemon peel**
  Lemon twists (optional)

Peel pears and remove cores (see photo 1). Enlarge openings slightly (see photo 2). Place pears in a 10x6x2-inch baking dish. Combine preserves and almonds. Fill centers of pears with preserves-nut mixture (see photo 4).

For sauce, in a small saucepan combine wine, crème de cassis, sugar, and lemon peel. Bring to boiling. Pour mixture over pears. Bake, uncovered, in a 350° oven about 45 minutes or till pears are just tender, basting several times with sauce (see photo 5). Serve fruit warm or chilled, with sauce. If desired, garnish with lemon twists. Makes 4 servings.

Microwave Directions: Prepare pears and filling as above. Place pears in a nonmetal 10x6x2-inch baking dish. Fill with preserves-nut mixture. Combine ingredients for sauce in a 2-cup glass measure. Micro-cook, uncovered, on 100% power (HIGH) about 1 minute or till mixture is boiling. Stir to dissolve sugar. Pour over pears. Micro-cook, covered, on 100% power (HIGH) for 7 to 8 minutes or till pears are just tender, giving dish a quarter-turn after 3 and 6 minutes and basting with sauce. Serve as above.

4 Place fruit in the baking dish, then combine the filling mixture. Use a small spoon to fill the hollowed-out fruit centers, dividing the mixture evenly.

5 To test the fruit for doneness, use a fork to poke the fruit. The fruit is done when it's just tender when tested with the fork.

Old-Fashioned Cobblers

As well-loved today as they were in the old days, cobblers have pleased generations of sweet tooths. What gives this old-fashioned favorite its top rating? It's the wonderful flavor that comes from teaming fruit filling with a stir-together biscuit topper.

Taste one of these cobblers. We think you'll agree that such tried-and-true desserts helped make the good old days so good.

Cherry-Berry
Cobbler

Cherry-Berry Cobbler

1   **10-ounce package frozen red raspberries, thawed**
1   **16-ounce package frozen unsweetened pitted tart red cherries, thawed**
½   **cup all-purpose flour**
½   **cup whole wheat flour**
3   **tablespoons sugar**
1½ **teaspoons baking powder**
¼   **teaspoon salt**
¼   **cup butter *or* margarine**
1   **egg**
⅓   **cup milk**
½   **cup sugar**
2   **tablespoons cornstarch**
1   **tablespoon sugar**
¼   **teaspoon ground cinnamon**
    Light cream

Drain raspberries, reserving syrup. If necessary, add enough water to raspberry syrup to measure ¾ cup liquid. (Do not drain cherries.) Set fruit and syrup aside.

In a mixing bowl stir together all-purpose flour, whole wheat flour, 3 tablespoons sugar, baking powder, and salt (see photo 1, page 16). Cut in butter or margarine till the mixture resembles coarse crumbs (see photo 1, page 12). Beat egg slightly; combine with milk. Set aside.

In a medium saucepan combine ½ cup sugar and cornstarch. Stir in reserved raspberry liquid and cherries with their liquid. Cook and stir over medium heat till thickened and bubbly. Gently stir in raspberries. Heat through, then reduce heat and keep hot (see photo 1).

Add egg-milk mixture all at once to dry ingredients, stirring just till mixture is moistened (see photo 2). Transfer hot cherry-raspberry mixture to a 2-quart casserole. *Immediately* spoon biscuit topping into 8 mounds onto *hot* fruit mixture (see photo 3). Stir together 1 tablespoon sugar and cinnamon; sprinkle atop the biscuit mounds. Bake in a 400° oven about 20 minutes or till topping tests done (see photo 4). Serve warm with light cream. Makes 8 servings.

1 Do as much of the measuring and combining of ingredients as you can before preparing the fruit mixture so you can mix it quickly. Then, fix the fruit and keep it hot over low heat while you finish stirring the topping ingredients together.

2 For the biscuit topping, add liquid ingredients to the dry ingredients, then stir just till moistened. Be careful not to overmix or the topping will be tough and will have a heavy texture.

3 Drop the topping in mounds onto the fruit filling. Be sure to keep the fruit mixture hot before adding the topping. This helps the topping to bake evenly.

4 To test the topping for doneness, insert a toothpick into the center of a mound. The pick should come out clean. If topping is doughy, continue baking a few minutes more.

The same toothpick test works when checking cakes for doneness.

Blueberry Cobbler

Good for all seasons! In the summer, use fresh berries—other times of the year use the frozen ones.

¾ **cup all-purpose flour**
2 **tablespoons sugar**
1 **teaspoon baking powder**
¼ **teaspoon ground nutmeg**
⅛ **teaspoon salt**
3 **tablespoons butter or margarine**
2 **cups fresh or frozen blueberries**
½ **cup water**
¼ **cup packed brown sugar**
2 **teaspoons lemon juice**
1 **tablespoon cold water**
2 **teaspoons cornstarch**
¼ **cup milk**
 Lemon yogurt (optional)

In a mixing bowl stir together flour, sugar, baking powder, nutmeg, and salt (see photo 1, page 16). Cut in butter or margarine till the mixture resembles coarse crumbs (see photo 1, page 12). Set aside.

In a medium saucepan combine blueberries, ½ cup water, brown sugar, and lemon juice. Bring to boiling, stirring occasionally. Combine 1 tablespoon water and cornstarch; stir into blueberry mixture. Cook and stir till thickened and bubbly. Reduce heat and keep blueberry mixture hot (see photo 1, page 26).

Add milk all at once to dry ingredients, stirring just till mixture is moistened (see photo 2, page 26). Transfer hot berry mixture to a 1½-quart casserole. *Immediately* spoon biscuit topping into 4 mounds onto *hot* fruit mixture in casserole (see photo 3, page 27).

Bake in a 400° oven about 20 minutes or till topping tests done (see photo 4, page 27). Serve warm. Dollop each serving with yogurt, if desired. Makes 4 servings.

Spicy Pineapple Cobbler

We've kept the calories down to only 203 per serving, without sacrificing flavor, by using juice-pack pineapple and very little sugar and fat.

½ **cup all-purpose flour**
2 **tablespoons sugar**
1 **teaspoon baking powder**
⅛ **teaspoon ground ginger**
1 **tablespoon butter or margarine**
½ **cup orange juice**
4 **teaspoons cornstarch**
1 **15¼-ounce can pineapple tidbits (juice pack)**
¼ **teaspoon pumpkin pie spice or ground cinnamon**
¼ **cup buttermilk**

In a mixing bowl stir together flour, sugar, baking powder, and ginger (see photo 1, page 16). Cut in butter or margarine till the mixture resembles coarse crumbs (see photo 1, page 12). Set mixture aside.

In a medium saucepan combine orange juice and cornstarch. Stir in *undrained* pineapple and pie spice or cinnamon. Cook and stir over medium heat till thickened and bubbly. Reduce heat and keep hot (see photo 1, page 26).

Add buttermilk all at once to dry ingredients, stirring just till mixture is moistened (see photo 2, page 26). Transfer hot pineapple mixture to a 1-quart casserole. *Immediately* spoon biscuit topping into 4 mounds onto *hot* fruit mixture (see photo 3, page 27). Bake in a 400° oven about 25 minutes or till topping tests done (see photo 4, page 27). Makes 4 servings.

Pear-Cranberry Cobbler

Graham crackers and nuts are surprise ingredients in the topping.

⅓ cup all-purpose flour
¼ cup whole wheat flour
¼ cup finely crushed graham crackers
2 tablespoons chopped walnuts
2 tablespoons brown sugar
1½ teaspoons baking powder
3 tablespoons butter *or* margarine
¾ cup cranberry juice cocktail
⅓ cup sugar
1½ cups sliced peeled pears (2 medium)
¾ cup cranberries
1 tablespoon cornstarch
1 tablespoon cold water
¼ cup milk
  Whipped cream

In a mixing bowl stir together all-purpose flour, whole wheat flour, graham crackers, walnuts, brown sugar, and baking powder (see photo 1, page 16). Cut in butter or margarine till the mixture resembles coarse crumbs (see photo 1, page 12). Set aside.

In a medium saucepan combine cranberry juice cocktail and sugar. Stir in pears and cranberries. Bring to boiling, stirring occasionally. Reduce heat; simmer, uncovered, 3 minutes. Combine cornstarch and water; stir into pear mixture. Cook and stir till thickened and bubbly. Reduce heat and keep hot (see photo 1, page 26).

Add milk all at once to dry ingredients, stirring just till mixture is moistened (see photo 2, page 26). Transfer hot fruit mixture to a 10x6x2-inch dish. *Immediately* spoon the biscuit topping into 4 mounds onto the *hot* fruit mixture (see photo 3, page 27).

Bake in a 400° oven about 15 minutes or till topping tests done (see photo 4, page 27). Serve warm with whipped cream. Serves 4.

Easy-as-Pie Cobbler

2 20-ounce cans apple pie filling
½ cup raisins
½ cup orange juice
1 tablespoon lemon juice
1 7-ounce package bran muffin mix
  Light cream *or* milk

In a medium saucepan combine pie filling, raisins, orange juice, and lemon juice. Bring to boiling, stirring occasionally. Meanwhile, prepare muffin mix according to package directions, *except* use *half* of the liquid called for on package. Transfer the hot apple mixture to a 12x7½x2-inch baking dish. *Immediately* spoon the muffin mixture into 8 mounds onto *hot* fruit mixture (see photo 3, page 27). Bake in a 400° oven about 20 minutes (see photo 4, page 27). Serve warm with cream. Makes 8 servings.

Microwave Directions: In a 3-quart nonmetal casserole combine pie filling, raisins, and juices. Micro-cook, covered, on 100% power (HIGH) for 9 to 10 minutes or till boiling, stirring *every* 3 minutes. Meanwhile, prepare muffin mix according to package directions, *except* use *half* of the liquid called for. *Immediately* spoon the muffin mixture into 8 mounds onto *hot* fruit mixture. Micro-cook, uncovered, on 100% power (HIGH) for 6 to 8 minutes. Give dish a half-turn *every* 2 minutes. Serve as above.

Attention, Microwave Owners!

Recipes with microwave directions were tested in countertop microwave ovens that operate on 600 to 700 watts. Times are approximate because microwave ovens vary by manufacturer.

Bake a Cake

Looking for new flavor twists on old favorites? Check out the next few pages of cakes.

For our spanking new tube cake, we've added a chocolate-peanut butter tunnel to a cake already chock-full of peanuts. And that's only one idea!

Discover other up-to-the-minute recipes, each a cake favorite turned into a new taste sensation.

Chocolate Tunnel Peanut Cake

Chocolate Tunnel Peanut Cake

2½ **cups all-purpose flour**
1 **teaspoon baking powder**
½ **teaspoon baking soda**
¾ **cup butter *or* margarine**
1⅓ **cups sugar**
½ **teaspoon vanilla**
3 **eggs**
1 **cup milk**
½ **cup chocolate-flavored syrup**
¼ **cup peanut butter**
½ **cup chopped peanuts**
  Peanut Butter Glaze

Generously grease and lightly flour a 10-inch fluted tube pan or 10-inch tube pan (see photos 1 and 2). Combine flour, baking powder, soda, and ¼ teaspoon *salt* (see photo 1, page 16).

In a large mixer bowl beat butter or margarine with an electric mixer on medium speed for 30 seconds. Add sugar and vanilla; beat till fluffy (see photo 2, page 16). Add eggs, one at a time, beating well after each (see photo 3). Add flour mixture and milk alternately to beaten mixture, beating on low speed after each addition just till combined (see photo 3, page 16).

Reserve *2 cups* of batter. Stir chocolate-flavored syrup and peanut butter together till well combined, then add to reserved batter; set aside. Stir peanuts into remaining batter and turn into the prepared pan, spreading evenly (see photo 4). Using the back of a spoon, make a slight indentation in the top of the batter around the center tube halfway between center and edge. Spoon chocolate batter into the indentation (see photo 5). Bake in a 350° oven for 50 to 55 minutes or till cake tests done (see photo 4, page 27). Cool in the pan on a wire rack for 10 minutes (see photo 6). Turn cake out of the pan onto a rack. Cool thoroughly. Drizzle Peanut Butter Glaze over top of cake. Makes 12 servings.

Peanut Butter Glaze: Combine 1 cup sifted *powdered sugar* and 2 tablespoons *peanut butter*. Add 1 to 2 tablespoons *milk* to make glaze of drizzling consistency.

1 Use shortening on a paper towel, a piece of waxed paper, or a pastry brush to grease the pan. When baking in a fluted pan, be sure to get shortening into all crevices—even in pans with nonstick coating.

2 Add a couple of tablespoons of flour to the well-greased pan. Tilt and tap the pan to evenly distribute the flour. Dump out any extra flour.

3 Break one egg at a time into a custard cup, then add it to the creamed mixture. Any shell fragments can easily be removed when the egg is first broken into the custard cup.

Beat the mixture after each egg addition until well combined; scrape the sides of the mixer bowl occasionally.

4 Pour the batter into the prepared pan, scraping the bowl. Spread the batter evenly in the pan with a rubber spatula, as shown. Make sure batter gets into all the corners of the pan.

5 Spoon the chocolate-flavored batter into the indentation, as shown. Don't spread or stir the two batters together. When baked, the chocolate-flavored batter forms a tunnel in the white batter.

6 Transfer the baked cake to a wire cooling rack. The rack allows air to circulate freely around and, most importantly, underneath the cake. Cooling a cake without elevating it on a rack will result in a gummy bottom layer on the cake.

Cocoa Streusel Cake

⅓ cup all-purpose flour
¼ cup packed brown sugar
3 tablespoons butter *or* margarine
½ of a 6-ounce package (½ cup)
    semisweet chocolate pieces
¼ cup chopped nuts
1¼ cups all-purpose flour
¼ cup unsweetened cocoa powder
¾ teaspoon baking soda
⅓ cup shortening
1 cup sugar
1 teaspoon vanilla
1 egg

Grease and lightly flour a 9x9x2-inch baking pan (see photos 1 and 2, page 32). For topping, combine ⅓ cup flour and brown sugar. Cut in butter or margarine till crumbly (see photo 1, page 12). Stir in chocolate and nuts; set aside.

For cake, stir together 1¼ cups flour, cocoa powder, baking soda, and ¼ teaspoon *salt* (see photo 1, page 16). In a small mixer bowl beat shortening with an electric mixer on medium speed for 30 seconds. Add sugar and vanilla; beat till well mixed. Add egg, beating well (see photo 3, page 32). Add flour mixture and ⅔ cup *water* alternately to beaten mixture, beating on low speed after each addition just till combined (see photo 3, page 16).

Pour *half* of the batter into the prepared pan, spreading evenly (see photo 4, page 32). Sprinkle *half* of the topping mixture over batter. Top with remaining batter and sprinkle with remaining topping mixture. Bake in a 350° oven for 30 to 35 minutes or till cake tests done (see photo 4, page 27). Cool cake in pan on a wire rack (see photo 6, page 33). Makes 9 servings.

Streusel Cupcakes: Prepare topping and batter as above. Line muffin pans with paper bake cups. Place *2 slightly rounded tablespoons* cake batter in each cup and top with *1 tablespoon* topping. Bake in a 350° oven for 15 to 20 minutes or till done. Remove to wire rack to cool. Makes about 24.

Lemony Carrot Cake

Instead of using spices, we've flavored the carrot cake favorite with citrus.

1¼ cups all-purpose flour
½ teaspoon baking powder
½ teaspoon baking soda
½ teaspoon salt
⅓ cup butter *or* margarine
1 cup sugar
1 teaspoon finely shredded lemon peel
1 teaspoon vanilla
2 eggs
¼ cup milk
1½ cups finely shredded carrot
    Lemon Frosting

Grease and lightly flour a 9x9x2-inch baking pan (see photos 1 and 2, page 32). Stir together flour, baking powder, baking soda, and salt (see photo 1, page 16). In a large mixer bowl beat butter or margarine with an electric mixer on medium speed for 30 seconds. Add sugar, lemon peel, and vanilla; beat till well mixed. Add eggs, one at a time, beating well after each (see photo 3, page 32). Add flour mixture and milk alternately to beaten mixture, beating on low speed after each addition just till combined (see photo 3, page 16). Stir in carrot.

Pour batter into the prepared pan, spreading evenly (see photo 4, page 32). Bake in a 350° oven about 30 minutes or till cake tests done (see photo 4, page 27). Cool cake in pan on a wire rack (see photo 6, page 33). Spread cooled cake with Lemon Frosting. Makes 9 servings.

Lemon Frosting: In a small mixer bowl beat 2 tablespoons *butter or margarine* till softened. Gradually add 1 cup sifted *powdered sugar,* beating well. Beat in ¼ teaspoon finely shredded *lemon peel* and ¼ teaspoon *vanilla.* Add enough *milk* (1 to 2 tablespoons) to make frosting spreadable.

Topsy-Turvy Spice Cake

Take an old-fashioned upside-down cake ... spice it up ... and make it with pears. The result? A new creation to serve for dessert.

3 tablespoons butter *or* margarine
½ cup packed brown sugar
¼ teaspoon ground cinnamon
1 8½-ounce can pear slices, drained
1½ cups all-purpose flour
½ teaspoon baking soda
½ teaspoon ground nutmeg
½ teaspoon ground cinnamon
⅛ teaspoon ground cloves
½ cup butter *or* margarine
½ cup sugar
½ cup molasses
1 egg
½ cup milk
Whipped cream (optional)

In a small saucepan melt 3 tablespoons butter or margarine. Stir in brown sugar and ¼ teaspoon cinnamon. Remove from heat. Spread mixture evenly in an 8x8x2-inch baking pan. Arrange pear slices in brown sugar mixture in the baking pan; set aside.

For batter, stir together flour, baking soda, nutmeg, ½ teaspoon cinnamon, and cloves (see photo 1, page 16). In a small mixer bowl beat ½ cup butter or margarine with an electric mixer on medium speed for 30 seconds. Add sugar; beat till fluffy (see photo 2, page 16). Add molasses and egg, beating well (see photo 3, page 32). (Mixture will appear curdled.) Add flour mixture and milk alternately to beaten mixture, beating on low speed after each addition just till combined (see photo 3, page 16).

Pour batter over pears in the pan, spreading evenly (see photo 4, page 32). Bake in a 350° oven for 40 to 45 minutes or till cake tests done (see photo 4, page 27). Cool in pan on a wire rack for 5 minutes (see photo 6, page 33). Invert onto a serving plate. Serve cake warm with whipped cream, if desired. Serves 9.

Tropical Topped Cake

Put some fruit in a broiled-on coconut topping for an old favorite with a new twist.

1 8-ounce can crushed pineapple (juice pack)
2½ cups all-purpose flour
1 tablespoon baking powder
½ cup shortening
¾ cup sugar
¾ cup packed brown sugar
1 teaspoon vanilla
2 eggs
⅓ cup packed brown sugar
3 tablespoons butter *or* margarine
1 tablespoon milk
1 cup coconut
¼ cup chopped walnuts
Whipped cream (optional)

Grease and lightly flour a 13x9x2-inch baking pan (see photos 1 and 2, page 32). Drain pineapple well, reserving juice. Add water to equal 1¼ cups liquid. Stir together flour, baking powder, and ½ teaspoon *salt* (see photo 1, page 16). In a large mixer bowl beat shortening with an electric mixer on medium speed for 30 seconds. Add sugar, ¾ cup brown sugar, and vanilla; beat till well mixed. Add eggs, one at a time, beating well after each (see photo 3, page 32).

Add flour mixture and reserved pineapple juice alternately to beaten mixture, beating on low speed after each addition just till combined (see photo 3, page 16). Pour batter into the prepared pan, spreading evenly (see photo 4, page 32). Bake in a 350° oven for 25 to 30 minutes or till cake tests done (see photo 4, page 27).

Meanwhile, in a small mixer bowl beat ⅓ cup brown sugar and butter or margarine till fluffy. Beat in milk. Stir in coconut, walnuts, and drained pineapple. Spread mixture over warm cake in pan. Broil 4 to 5 inches from heat about 3 minutes or till golden brown. Cool cake in pan on a wire rack about 20 minutes (see photo 6, page 33). Serve warm or cool with whipped cream, if desired. Makes 12 to 15 servings.

Strawberry Ice Cream

Homemade Ice Creams

For a fun-to-eat dessert, ice cream is the perfect choice, especially when it's turned out of an ice cream freezer.

You can spoon it from a dish, lick it out of a cone, or make it into a sundae. Anyway you choose to eat it, homemade ice cream is a special taste treat that's hard to resist.

Chocolate Ice Cream

Easy Vanilla Ice Cream

Easy Vanilla Ice Cream

2 **eggs**
4 **cups whipping cream**
3 **cups light cream**
2 **cups sugar**
1 **tablespoon vanilla**
Crushed ice
Rock salt

In a large mixing bowl beat eggs. Stir in whipping cream, light cream, sugar, and vanilla. Stir till sugar is dissolved. Pour mixture into the freezer can of a 4- or 5-quart ice cream freezer (see photo 1). Fit can into the outer freezer bucket. Add the dasher, then cover with the freezer can lid.

Fit the motor or crank into place. Turn the motor on, then alternate layers of ice and salt in the outer freezer bucket (see photo 2). Freeze till done according to manufacturer's directions, adding ice and salt occasionally as ice melts. Unplug freezer. Carefully drain off the water through drain hole in outer freezer bucket. Remove motor or crank and dasher (see photo 3).

Cover the can with the lid and repack with ice and salt (see tip, page 40). Ripen ice cream for 4 hours (see photo 4). Makes 3 quarts.

Chocolate Ice Cream: Prepare Easy Vanilla Ice Cream as above, *except* stir 1 cup *chocolate-flavored syrup* into eggs before adding whipping cream. Freeze as directed. Makes 3 quarts.

Strawberry Ice Cream: Thaw one 10-ounce package frozen *sliced strawberries;* finely crush berries. Prepare Easy Vanilla Ice Cream as above, *except* stir in strawberries with whipping cream. Freeze as directed. Makes 3 quarts.

Chocolate Chip Ice Cream: Prepare Easy Vanilla Ice Cream as above, *except* stir in one 6-ounce package (1 cup) *miniature semisweet chocolate pieces* with whipping cream. Freeze as directed. Makes 3 quarts.

1 Pour the cold ice cream mixture into the freezer can of a 4- or 5-quart ice cream freezer. The can should be no more than ⅔ full. This allows room for the ice cream to expand as air is beaten in with the dasher.

  Place the ice cream freezer where it can drain during freezing.

2 Start the freezer motor before alternately adding layers of ice and salt. Follow manufacturer's directions for amounts. (*Or,* use 6 cups crushed ice to 1 cup rock salt.) If you pack the ice and salt before the freezer is started, ice pieces can become wedged so that the freezer can is unable to turn freely. Add cold water with ice following the manufacturer's directions.

3 Before opening the can, make sure ice and salt are below the level of the can lid so that no melted ice seeps into the can. Wipe the can and lid.

Leaving freezer can in the bucket, remove the dasher. Scrape dasher using a rubber spatula or spoon.

4 To ripen ice cream, see tip, page 40. Then cover the ice- and salt-packed ice cream freezer with a heavy cloth or layers of newspaper to keep the contents cold. Drain off water and add extra salt and ice as necessary during ripening. Ripening allows ice cream to harden slightly and become smoother.

To serve, uncover and remove ice and salt to below level of the can lid. Wipe off can and lid before opening the can.

Banana-Pecan Ice Cream

2 eggs
2 cups whipping cream
1 12-ounce can (1½ cups) evaporated milk
1 cup sugar
1½ teaspoons vanilla
2 ripe medium bananas, mashed (⅔ cup)
½ cup chopped pecans, toasted
Crushed ice
Rock salt

In a large mixing bowl beat eggs. Stir in cream, milk, sugar, and vanilla; stir till sugar is dissolved. Stir in bananas and nuts. Pour mixture into the freezer can of a 4- or 5-quart ice cream freezer (see photo 1, page 38). Fit can into the outer freezer bucket. Add the dasher, then cover with the freezer can lid.

Fit the motor or crank into place. Turn the motor on, then alternate layers of ice and salt in the outer freezer bucket (see photo 2, page 38). Freeze till done according to manufacturer's directions, adding ice and salt occasionally as ice melts. Unplug freezer. Carefully drain off water through drain hole in outer freezer bucket. Remove motor or crank and dasher (see photo 3, page 39). Cover can with lid and repack with ice and salt (see tip box, below). Ripen for 4 hours (see photo 4, page 39). Makes 2 quarts.

Ripening

After removing dasher, cover freezer can with waxed paper or foil. Plug hole in lid before replacing lid on can. Pack outer freezer bucket with ice and salt, covering top of ice cream can. Follow manufacturer's directions for proportions. (*Or,* use 4 cups ice per 1 cup rock salt.)

Ginger-Raisin Ice Cream

According to Marcia, a taste panel member, this ice cream, "tastes like a ginger cookie!"

½ cup raisins, chopped
2 tablespoons rum
3 eggs
3 cups whipping cream
2 cups milk
¾ cup sugar
1 tablespoon light molasses
1 tablespoon vanilla
2 cups broken gingersnap cookies (about 20 cookies)
Crushed ice
Rock salt

In a small bowl combine raisins and rum; set aside. Meanwhile, in an extra-large mixing bowl beat eggs. Stir in cream, milk, sugar, molasses, and vanilla; stir till sugar is dissolved. Stir in *1 cup* of the cookies and raisin mixture. Pour mixture into the freezer can of a 4- or 5-quart ice cream freezer (see photo 1, page 38). Fit can into the outer freezer bucket. Add the dasher, then cover with the freezer can lid.

Fit the motor or crank into place. Turn the motor on, then alternate layers of ice and salt in the outer freezer bucket (see photo 2, page 38). Freeze until done according to manufacturer's directions, adding ice and salt occasionally as ice melts. Unplug freezer. Carefully drain off water through drain hole in outer freezer bucket. Remove motor or crank and dasher (see photo 3, page 39). Stir in remaining cookies.

Cover the can with the lid and repack with ice and salt (see tip, left). Ripen ice cream for 4 hours (see photo 4, page 39). Makes 2½ quarts.

Apple Pie Ice Cream

Use kitchen scissors to easily cut up apples in pie filling. Save a bowl and do the cutting right in the can.

1¼	cups sugar
2	envelopes unflavored gelatin
2	cups milk
4	eggs
4	cups light cream
1	4-serving-size package *instant* vanilla pudding mix
1	tablespoon lemon juice
¾	teaspoon ground cinnamon
¼	teaspoon ground nutmeg
1	20-ounce can apple pie filling, cut up
	Crushed ice
	Rock salt

In a medium saucepan combine sugar and gelatin. Stir in milk. Stir over low heat till gelatin and sugar are dissolved. In a large mixing bowl beat eggs. Stir in cream, pudding mix, lemon juice, cinnamon, and nutmeg till mixed. Stir in milk-gelatin mixture and pie filling. Chill several hours. Pour mixture into the freezer can of a 4- or 5-quart ice cream freezer (see photo 1, page 38). Fit can into the outer freezer bucket. Add the dasher, then cover with the freezer can lid.

Fit the motor or crank into place. Turn the motor on, then alternate layers of crushed ice and rock salt in the outer freezer bucket (see photo 2, page 38). Freeze till done according to manufacturer's directions, adding ice and salt occasionally as ice melts. Unplug freezer. Carefully drain off water through drain hole in outer freezer bucket. Remove motor or crank and dasher (see photo 3, page 39).

Cover the can with the lid and repack with ice and salt (see tip, page 40). Ripen ice cream for 4 hours (see photo 4, page 39). Makes about 3 quarts ice cream.

Ice Cream Toppers

For the crowning touch, add a topping to homemade ice cream.

Fudge Sauce: In a small, heavy saucepan combine one 6-ounce package *semisweet chocolate pieces,* one 5-ounce can (⅔ cup) *evaporated milk,* ¼ cup *light corn syrup* or *creamy peanut butter,* and 1 tablespoon *butter.* Stir over low heat till chocolate is melted. Stir in 1 teaspoon *vanilla.* Serve warm. Makes 1⅓ cups.

Marshmallow Topping: Heat ⅓ cup *light corn syrup* and 2 tablespoons *water* till boiling. Remove from heat. Stir in ½ cup *tiny marshmallows,* ¼ teaspoon *vanilla,* and few drops *almond extract;* stir till marshmallows are melted. Beat 1 *egg white* and ¼ teaspoon *cream of tartar* till stiff peaks form. Gradually add marshmallow mixture, beating till mixture mounds when spooned. Use immediately. Chill leftovers for a few days. Stir before using. Makes 2 cups.

Praline Sauce: In a heavy saucepan combine ¾ cup *sugar,* ¾ cup packed *brown sugar,* ½ cup *light cream,* and 3 tablespoons *butter.* Cook over medium-high heat till boiling; stir constantly to dissolve sugars. Reduce heat. Cook and stir 5 minutes more or till slightly thickened. Stir in ½ cup chopped *pecans.* Serve warm. Makes 1⅔ cups.

Stack a Shortcake

What makes a shortcake "short" even though it's stacked so high? The "short" comes from the high proportion of shortening in the biscuit-like cake. Start with this luscious biscuit base. Then, build the stack with a filling between and on top.

You've just created a shortcake treat that's plenty long on flavor.

Chocolate-Nectarine Shortcake

Chocolate-Nectarine Shortcake

6 **medium nectarines, pitted and sliced (about 4 cups)**
¼ **cup sugar**
1⅔ **cups all-purpose flour**
½ **cup sugar**
⅓ **cup unsweetened cocoa powder**
2 **teaspoons baking powder**
¼ **teaspoon baking soda**
½ **cup butter *or* margarine**
1 **beaten egg**
⅔ **cup milk**
1 **cup whipping cream**
2 **tablespoons sugar**
½ **teaspoon vanilla**

In a bowl toss nectarines and ¼ cup sugar together; set aside.

Meanwhile, grease a 9x1½-inch round baking pan; set aside. In a mixing bowl stir together flour, ½ cup sugar, cocoa powder, baking powder, and baking soda. Cut in butter or margarine till mixture resembles coarse crumbs (see photo 1, page 12). In a bowl stir together egg and milk. Add mixture all at once to dry ingredients and stir just till moistened (see photo 2, page 26).

Spread shortcake dough in the prepared pan (see photo 1). Bake in a 450° oven for 15 to 20 minutes or till done (do not overbake). Cool in the pan on a wire rack for 10 minutes. Remove shortcake from the pan.

Beat whipping cream, 2 tablespoons sugar, and vanilla (see photo 2). Split warm shortcake into two layers, then carefully lift off top layer (see photo 3). Assemble shortcake by spooning nectarines and whipped cream between shortcake layers and over the top (see photo 4). If desired, garnish with a nectarine slice. Serve warm. Makes 8 servings.

1 For one shortcake, use a rubber spatula to evenly spread the dough in the greased baking pan. Build up the edges slightly so that as the cake bakes, the center will rise to the same level as the sides. For individual shortcakes, drop the dough into 8 mounds on a baking sheet.

2 Use an electric mixer or a rotary beater to beat the whipping cream, sugar, and vanilla together. To get the best volume, use chilled cream and chill the utensils about 30 minutes in the refrigerator or about 10 minutes in the freezer.

Beat cream until it mounds slightly and soft peaks form when the beaters are removed. Avoid overbeating, or the whipping cream will turn to butter.

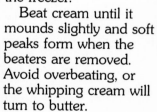

3 To split the short-cake, first insert toothpicks halfway up the side of the warm shortcake to use as a cutting guide. Cut the shortcake in half horizontally with a sharp, long-bladed knife. Remove picks as you cut.

Carefully lift off the top layer with a wide spatula or two narrow spatulas.

Individual shortcakes are easily split in half with a sharp knife.

4 Spoon a portion of the fruit mixture over bottom layer, as shown. Then, add the whipped cream. Replace shortcake top. Add additional fruit. To keep the whipped cream from melting on the warm shortcake, spoon directly onto the fruit.

Apple-Orange Shortcakes

1	orange
3	tablespoons butter *or* margarine
2	apples, peeled, cored, and sliced
2	tablespoons sugar
¼	teaspoon ground cinnamon
½	cup orange juice
1	teaspoon cornstarch
1	cup all-purpose flour
2	teaspoons sugar
1½	teaspoons baking powder
¼	teaspoon salt
¼	cup shortening
½	cup milk
½	cup whipping cream
2	tablespoons chopped pecans

Finely shred orange peel to make ½ teaspoon, then section orange; set aside. In a medium saucepan melt butter or margarine. Add apples, 2 tablespoons sugar, and cinnamon. Cook, uncovered, over medium heat about 5 minutes or till apples are just tender; gently stir often. Stir together orange juice and cornstarch; add to apple mixture. Cook and stir till thickened and bubbly. Reduce heat, then cook and stir 2 minutes more. Stir in orange sections; cool.

Meanwhile, lightly grease a baking sheet; set aside (see photo 1, page 32). In a mixing bowl stir together flour, 2 teaspoons sugar, baking powder, salt, and orange peel (see photo 1, page 16). Cut in shortening till mixture resembles coarse crumbs (see photo 1, page 12). Add milk all at once to dry ingredients and stir just till dough clings together. Drop dough into 4 mounds on the prepared baking sheet (see photo 1, page 44). Bake in a 425° oven about 12 minutes or till golden.

Beat whipping cream (see photo 2, page 44). Split warm individual shortcakes in half (see photo 3, page 45). Assemble shortcakes in individual dessert dishes by spooning fruit mixture between shortcake layers and over the tops (see photo 4, page 45). Sprinkle nuts on top. Serve warm with whipped cream. Makes 4 servings.

Easy Fruit-Yogurt Shortcake

Match the fresh fruit garnish with the yogurt flavor you choose—sliced strawberries with strawberry yogurt and sliced peaches or nectarines with the peach yogurt.

1½	cups packaged pancake mix
3	tablespoons brown sugar
¼	cup shortening
1	beaten egg
2	8-ounce cartons strawberry *or* peach yogurt
⅓	cup milk
1	4-ounce container frozen whipped dessert topping, thawed
	Fresh fruit (optional)

Grease an 8x1½-inch round baking pan; set aside (see photo 1, page 32). In a mixing bowl stir together pancake mix and sugar (see photo 1, page 16). Cut in shortening till mixture resembles coarse crumbs (see photo 1, page 12). In a bowl stir together egg, ½ *cup* of yogurt, and milk. Add egg mixture all at once to dry ingredients and stir mixture just till moistened (see photo 2, page 26).

Spread shortcake dough in the prepared pan (see photo 1, page 44). Bake in a 450° oven for 15 to 18 minutes or till done (do not overbake). Cool in the pan on a wire rack for 10 minutes. Remove shortcake from the pan. Cool thoroughly on the rack.

For topping, fold remaining yogurt into dessert topping till smooth. Split shortcake into two layers, then carefully lift off top layer (see photo 3, page 45). Assemble shortcake by spooning yogurt mixture between shortcake layers and over the top (see photo 4, page 45). Garnish with fresh fruit, if desired. Makes 6 servings.

Pear-Berry Nut Cake

½	cup sugar
½	teaspoon finely shredded lemon peel
1	tablespoon lemon juice
3	cups sliced peeled pears (about 6 pears)
4	teaspoons cornstarch
1	cup blueberries
2	cups all-purpose flour
2	tablespoons brown sugar
1	tablespoon baking powder
½	cup butter *or* margarine
1	beaten egg
¾	cup milk *or* light cream
½	cup finely chopped pecans
2	tablespoons orange liqueur
1	pint vanilla ice cream

In a medium saucepan stir together ½ cup sugar, lemon peel, lemon juice, and ¾ cup *water*. Bring to boiling, stirring to dissolve sugar. Add pears; bring to boiling. Reduce heat, then simmer, covered, about 3 minutes or till pears are tender. Combine cornstarch and ¼ cup *cold water*. Add to pear mixture. Cook and stir till thickened and bubbly. Reduce heat, then cook and stir 2 minutes more. Remove from heat. Stir in blueberries. Set aside.

Meanwhile, grease an 8x8x2-inch baking pan; set aside (see photo 1, page 32). In a mixing bowl stir together flour, brown sugar, and baking powder (see photo 1, page 16). Cut in butter or margarine till mixture resembles coarse crumbs (see photo 1, page 12). In a bowl stir together egg and milk or cream. Add egg mixture all at once to dry ingredients and stir just till moistened (see photo 2, page 26). Stir in nuts. Spread dough in the prepared pan (see photo 1, page 44). Bake in a 450° oven for 15 to 20 minutes or till done (do not overbake). Cool in pan on rack for 10 minutes. Remove from pan.

Split warm shortcake into two layers, then carefully lift off top layer (see photo 3, page 45). Drizzle orange liqueur over bottom layer. Assemble by spooning pear mixture between shortcake layers and over the top (see photo 4, page 45). Serve warm with ice cream. Serves 8.

Banana Split Shortcakes

A new twist on the old-fashioned strawberry favorite.

2½	cups sliced fresh strawberries
¼	cup sugar
1	cup all-purpose flour
3	tablespoons sugar
2	teaspoons baking powder
3	tablespoons butter *or* margarine
⅓	cup mashed ripe banana (1 medium)
3	tablespoons milk
½	cup whipping cream
2	tablespoons sugar
2	to 3 teaspoons unsweetened cocoa powder
	Sliced banana (optional)

In a bowl toss strawberries with ¼ cup sugar; set aside and allow berries to form juice.

Meanwhile, in a mixing bowl stir together flour, 3 tablespoons sugar, and baking powder (see photo 1, page 16). Cut in butter or margarine till mixture resembles coarse crumbs (see photo 1, page 12). In a bowl stir together mashed banana and milk. Add banana mixture all at once to dry ingredients and stir just till dough clings together. Drop dough into 5 mounds on an ungreased baking sheet (see photo 1, page 44). Bake in a 425° oven for 9 to 10 minutes or till golden.

Beat whipping cream, 2 tablespoons sugar, and cocoa powder (see photo 2, page 44). Split warm individual shortcakes in half (see photo 3, page 45). Assemble shortcakes in individual dessert dishes by spooning strawberries and whipped cream between shortcake layers and over the tops (see photo 4, page 45). Garnish with additional banana slices, if desired. Serve warm. Makes 5 servings.

Creamy Puddings

If the proof of the pudding is in the eating, here you'll find desserts that will prove to be delicious. These versatile recipes are perfect for both everyday meals and special occasions.

Top pudding with fruit or whipped cream for a family dessert. Or, gussy up that pudding: layer it with nuts and chocolate.

Dig into our puddings. You'll have the proof you need, right on your spoon.

Citrus Pudding Parfaits

Citrus Pudding Parfaits

4 medium oranges
¾ cup sugar
3 tablespoons cornstarch
2 beaten egg yolks
2 tablespoons butter *or* margarine
¼ cup coconut
¼ cup chopped pecans
½ of a 6-ounce package (½ cup) semisweet chocolate pieces
2 teaspoons shortening
Whipped cream (optional)
Chocolate curls (optional)

Finely shred ¾ teaspoon peel from orange; set aside. Squeeze juice from oranges; add water, if necessary, to measure 1¾ cups liquid. In a medium saucepan stir together sugar and cornstarch; stir in orange juice mixture (see photo 1). Cook and stir over medium heat till thickened and bubbly. Reduce heat, then cook and stir 2 minutes more. Remove from heat.

Gradually stir about *half* of the hot mixture into egg yolks (see photo 2). Return to mixture in saucepan and bring to a gentle boil (see photo 3). Reduce heat. Cook and stir 1 to 2 minutes more. Remove from heat. Stir in butter and orange peel. Pour mixture into a bowl. Cover surface with clear plastic wrap or waxed paper (see photo 4). Chill without stirring.

Meanwhile, in an 8x8x2-inch baking pan stir coconut and nuts together. Spread evenly in the pan. Bake in a 350° oven for 6 to 7 minutes or till lightly browned, stirring once or twice. Cool.

Just before serving, in a small heavy saucepan stir chocolate and shortening over low heat till chocolate begins to melt. Remove from heat; stir till smooth. Cool slightly. Layer pudding (about 2 tablespoons), melted chocolate (about ½ teaspoon), and coconut-nut mixture (about ½ tablespoon) in each of 4 parfait glasses; repeat layering two more times, ending with the coconut-nut mixture (see photo 5). Garnish with whipped cream and chocolate curls, if desired. Serve immediately. Makes 4 servings.

1 Thoroughly stir together the sugar and cornstarch in a saucepan so the cornstarch is evenly distributed. Then your pudding won't be lumpy. Add the liquid and stir until the dry and liquid ingredients are well combined.

2 Remove the saucepan from the heat. Then stir half of the hot mixture into the beaten yolks. This warms the eggs before they are added to the hot mixture in the saucepan.

If the eggs are added directly to the hot mixture, they will start to cook and you'll get pieces of cooked egg throughout the smooth pudding mixture.

3 After the egg yolks are added to the saucepan, return the mixture to a gentle boil. Cook and stir a few minutes longer to cook the yolks. If you are using whole eggs, bring mixture *almost* to boiling, but don't boil, or eggs will curdle.

4 Cover the surface of the hot pudding with clear plastic wrap or waxed paper. Place the piece of wrap directly on the surface of the hot pudding. This keeps a "skin" from forming on the pudding's surface.

5 Start layering pudding in each parfait glass, using a small spoon. Next comes a layer of melted chocolate, then coconut-nut mixture. Repeat layering with the rest of the ingredients, making three layers of pudding, chocolate, and coconut-nut mixture in each glass.

Versatile Vanilla Pudding

Not only can you serve the plain pudding or variations described below, you can also make sauce from this recipe by using just half of the thickening.

⅓ cup sugar
2 tablespoons cornstarch
   or ¼ cup all-purpose flour
   Dash salt
2¼ cups milk
2 beaten egg yolks *or* 1 beaten egg
1 tablespoon butter *or* margarine
1½ teaspoons vanilla

In a medium saucepan stir together sugar, cornstarch or flour, and salt; stir in milk (see photo 1, page 50). Cook and stir over medium heat till thickened and bubbly. Reduce heat, then cook and stir 2 minutes more. Remove from heat.

Gradually stir about *half* of the hot mixture into egg yolks or egg (see photo 2, page 50). Return to mixture in saucepan. If using egg yolks, bring to a gentle boil; if using whole egg, cook till nearly bubbly but *do not boil* (see photo 3, page 51). Reduce heat. Cook and stir 1 to 2 minutes more. Remove from heat. Stir in butter or margarine and vanilla. Pour mixture into a bowl. Cover surface with clear plastic wrap or waxed paper (see photo 4, page 51). Chill without stirring. To serve, spoon into dishes. Serves 4.

Tangy Vanilla Pudding: Prepare Versatile Vanilla Pudding as above, *except* omit butter or margarine. After chilling, fold in one 8-ounce carton *dairy sour cream or* one 8-ounce carton *plain yogurt.* Spoon into dishes. Serves 6.

Chocolate Pudding: Prepare Versatile Vanilla Pudding as above, *except* stir in ½ cup *semisweet chocolate pieces* with the milk. Continue as directed. Makes 4 servings.

Liqueur-Flavored Pudding: Prepare Versatile Vanilla Pudding as above, *except* omit the vanilla. Stir 2 tablespoons *orange liqueur or coffee liqueur* into cooked pudding with the butter or margarine. Continue as directed. Serves 4.

Microwave Directions: In a 1½-quart non-metal casserole stir together sugar, cornstarch or flour, and salt. Stir in milk. Micro-cook, uncovered, on 100% power (HIGH) for 6 to 8 minutes or till thickened and bubbly, stirring every minute till slightly thickened. Gradually stir about *half* of the hot mixture into egg yolks *(do not use 1 whole egg).* Return to mixture in casserole. Micro-cook, uncovered, on 100% power (HIGH) for 1½ to 2½ minutes or till bubbly; stir *every* 30 seconds. Stir in butter or margarine and vanilla. Continue as directed.

Hot Cocoa Pudding

½ cup sugar
¼ cup all-purpose flour
3 tablespoons unsweetened cocoa powder
   Dash salt
2 cups milk
1 beaten egg
1 tablespoon butter *or* margarine
1 teaspoon vanilla
½ cup tiny marshmallows (optional)

In a medium saucepan stir together sugar, flour, cocoa powder, and salt; stir in milk (see photo 1, page 50). Cook and stir over medium heat till thickened and bubbly. Reduce heat; cook and stir 1 minute more. Remove from heat.

Gradually stir about *half* of the hot mixture into egg (see photo 2, page 50). Return to mixture in saucepan. Cook and stir till nearly bubbly but *do not boil* (see photo 3, page 51). Reduce heat. Cook and stir 1 to 2 minutes more. Remove from heat. Stir in butter or margarine and vanilla. Fold in marshmallows, if desired.

Spoon into dessert dishes. Cover surface with clear plastic wrap or waxed paper (see photo 4, page 51). Serve warm or chilled. Serves 4.

Pumpkin Pudding

Instead of sinking your teeth into a piece of pumpkin pie, save calories by making this pumpkin dessert. It has about half the calories of pie.

½ **cup sugar**
3 **tablespoons cornstarch**
1 **teaspoon pumpkin pie spice**
2 **cups skim milk**
1 **cup canned pumpkin**
1 **beaten egg**
½ **teaspoon vanilla**
2 **tablespoons chopped walnuts**

In a medium saucepan stir together sugar, cornstarch, and pumpkin pie spice; stir in milk and pumpkin (see photo 1, page 50). Cook and stir over medium heat till thickened and bubbly. Reduce heat, then cook and stir 2 minutes more. Remove from heat.

Gradually stir about *half* of the hot mixture into egg (see photo 2, page 50). Return to mixture in saucepan. Cook and stir till nearly bubbly but *do not boil* (see photo 3, page 51). Reduce heat. Cook and stir 1 to 2 minutes more. Remove from heat. Stir in vanilla. Pour into 6 dessert dishes. Cover surface with clear plastic wrap or waxed paper (see photo 4, page 51). Chill without stirring. To serve, sprinkle pudding with nuts. Makes 6 servings.

Microwave Directions: In a 1½-quart nonmetal casserole stir together sugar, cornstarch, and spice. Stir in milk and pumpkin. Microcook, uncovered, on 100% power (HIGH) for 6 to 8 minutes or till thickened and bubbly, stirring every minute till slightly thickened. Substitute 2 well-beaten *egg yolks* for the 1 whole egg. Gradually stir about *half* of the hot mixture into yolks. Return to mixture in casserole. Microcook, uncovered, on 100% power (HIGH) for 2 to 3 minutes or till edges are bubbly, stirring every 30 seconds. Cook 30 seconds more. Stir in vanilla. Continue as directed.

Cheesecake Pudding Parfaits

Change the character of these parfaits by layering fresh or canned cut-up fruit between pudding layers instead of the crumb mixture.

⅓ **cup sugar**
2 **tablespoons all-purpose flour**
1¾ **cups milk**
1 **beaten egg**
1 **teaspoon vanilla**
1 **3-ounce package cream cheese, softened**
⅓ **cup dairy sour cream**
7 **graham cracker squares**
2 **tablespoons chopped pecans**
2 **tablespoons butter *or* margarine, melted**

In a medium saucepan stir together sugar and flour. Stir in milk (see photo 1, page 50). Cook and stir over medium heat till thickened and bubbly. Reduce heat, then cook and stir 1 minute more. Remove from heat.

Gradually stir about *half* of the hot mixture into egg (see photo 2, page 50). Return to mixture in saucepan. Cook and stir till nearly bubbly but *do not boil* (see photo 3, page 51). Reduce heat. Cook and stir 1 to 2 minutes more. Remove from heat. Stir in vanilla. Pour mixture into a bowl. Cut cream cheese into pieces and add to hot pudding. Stir till cheese is melted. Stir in sour cream. Cover surface with clear plastic wrap or waxed paper (see photo 4, page 51). Chill without stirring.

Meanwhile, crush graham crackers; measure ½ cup. In a mixing bowl toss together the ½ cup crushed crackers, nuts, and melted butter or margarine. To serve, layer pudding and crumbnut mixture in 4 parfait glasses; repeat layers, ending with crumb-nut mixture (see photo 5, page 51). Chill several hours, if desired, or serve immediately. Makes 4 servings.

Chilly Sherbets And Ices

Brrr. Whatever the weather, make your dessert forecast call for a cool treat.

In this chapter we shower you with a delicious selection of sherbets and ices. Their delectable flavors and low calorie counts will have you storming the kitchen for more.

Strawberry Sorbet

Strawberry Sorbet

You'll find just 101 calories per serving in this refreshing sorbet (sahr BEH).

1 pint fresh strawberries *or* raspberries
    (about 2 cups)
¾ cup orange juice
½ cup milk
¼ cup honey
2 egg whites
1 tablespoon honey

Remove hulls from berries. To a blender container add strawberries or raspberries, orange juice, milk, and ¼ cup honey. Cover, then blend about 1 minute or till smooth. (If desired, strain raspberry mixture to remove seeds.) Pour mixture into a 9x9x2-inch pan. Cover and freeze the mixture 2 to 3 hours or till almost firm.

In a small mixer bowl beat egg whites with an electric mixer on medium speed till soft peaks form (tips curl). Gradually add 1 tablespoon honey, beating on high speed till stiff peaks form (tips stand straight) (see photo 1).

Break frozen mixture into chunks (see photo 2). Transfer frozen mixture to a chilled large mixer bowl. Beat with an electric mixer till smooth but not melted (see photo 3). Fold in beaten egg whites (see photo 4). Return quickly to the cold pan. Cover and freeze 6 to 8 hours or till firm.

To serve, scrape across the frozen mixture with a spoon and mound in dessert dishes. If desired, serve sorbet over sliced fresh strawberries or orange sections. Makes 6 servings.

1 While the electric mixer is running, gradually add the honey or sugar to the partially beaten egg whites. The mixer should be set on high speed. Beat until the tips of the egg whites stand straight when the beaters are removed, as shown.

2 Using a spoon, break the frozen sorbet mixture into chunks. The frozen mixture should be firm, but not so solid that you can't break it up.

3 Transfer the chunks of frozen mixture to a chilled mixer bowl. The icy-cold bowl helps keep the mixture from melting too quickly.

Then, beat with an electric mixer until mixture is smooth, but *not* melted. The air that you beat in helps produce a frozen mixture with a smooth consistency.

4 To fold in the beaten egg whites, cut down through the mixture, go across the bottom of the bowl, then up and over the mixture close to the surface, as shown. A rubber spatula is a good utensil to use for folding.

Repeat the motion until the egg whites are thoroughly combined. Turn the bowl as you work. Don't overmix—the egg whites add air to the mixture; you don't want to lose the air by overmixing.

Honey-Grapefruit Ice

After a heavy meal, a light dessert with only 103 calories makes a perfect sweet ending. You're entertaining? Make the ice a week ahead.

2 **medium grapefruit**
1½ **cups water**
½ **cup honey**
1 **teaspoon finely shredded lemon peel**
3 **tablespoons lemon juice**
  Fresh mint leaves (optional)

Shred enough grapefruit peel to make 1 teaspoon. Squeeze grapefruit; measure 1 cup grapefruit juice. In a mixing bowl stir together water and honey; add shredded grapefruit peel, grapefruit juice, shredded lemon peel, and lemon juice. Stir till mixed. Pour grapefruit-lemon mixture into a 9x9x2-inch pan. Cover and freeze mixture for 3 to 4 hours or till almost firm.

Break frozen mixture into chunks (see photo 2, page 56). Transfer frozen mixture to a chilled large mixer bowl. Beat with an electric mixer till smooth but not melted (see photo 3, page 56). Return quickly to the cold pan. Cover and freeze for 6 to 8 hours or till firm.

To serve, let ice stand about 5 minutes at room temperature. Scrape across the frozen mixture with a spoon and mound in individual dessert dishes. If desired, garnish with mint leaves. Makes 6 to 8 servings.

Lime Sherbet

A refreshingly tart citrus treat.

⅔ **cup sugar**
1 **teaspoon unflavored gelatin**
1½ **cups milk**
1 **8-ounce carton vanilla yogurt**
1 **teaspoon finely shredded lime peel**
⅓ **cup lime juice**
  Finely shredded lime peel (optional)

In a medium saucepan stir together sugar and gelatin. Stir in milk. Stir over low heat till gelatin dissolves. Mix in yogurt, 1 teaspoon lime peel, and lime juice. Cool. Pour mixture into a 9x9x2-inch pan. Cover and freeze the mixture 2 to 3 hours or till almost firm.

Break frozen mixture into chunks (see photo 2, page 56). Transfer frozen mixture to a chilled large mixer bowl. Beat with an electric mixer till smooth but not melted (see photo 3, page 56). Return quickly to the cold pan. Cover and freeze about 3 hours or till firm.

To serve, let sherbet stand 10 to 15 minutes at room temperature. Scoop into dessert dishes. If desired, sprinkle with additional shredded lime peel. Makes 6 servings.

Kiwi Fruit Sherbet

Kiwi fruit are small, fuzzy, brown, oval-shaped fruit. They taste like ripe melon and give the sherbet a wonderfully sweet flavor.

1   **cup water**
½   **cup sugar**
4   **kiwi fruit, peeled**
½   **cup milk**
¼   **teaspoon finely shredded lime peel**
1   **tablespoon lime juice**
     Few drops green food coloring (optional)
2   **egg whites**
¼   **cup sugar**
1   **kiwi fruit (optional)**

In a small saucepan stir together water and ½ cup sugar. Bring to boiling, stirring to dissolve sugar. Cool. Cut up 4 kiwi fruit. To a blender container or food processor bowl add cut-up kiwi fruit and milk. Cover, then blend or process about 30 seconds or till smooth. Stir in lime peel, lime juice, food coloring, if desired, and cooled syrup mixture. Pour mixture into a 9x9x2-inch pan. Cover and freeze 2 to 3 hours or till almost firm.

In a small mixer bowl beat egg whites with an electric mixer on medium speed till soft peaks form (tips curl) (see photo 2, page 62). Gradually add ¼ cup sugar, beating till stiff peaks form (tips stand straight) (see photo 1, page 56).

Break frozen mixture into chunks (see photo 2, page 56). Transfer frozen mixture to a chilled large mixer bowl. Beat with an electric mixer till smooth but not melted (see photo 3, page 56). Fold in beaten egg whites (see photo 4, page 57). Return quickly to the cold pan. Cover and freeze about 3 hours or till firm.

To serve, let sherbet stand about 5 minutes at room temperature. Scoop into dessert dishes. If desired, garnish with a small wedge of kiwi fruit. Makes 6 servings.

Apricot-Orange Sherbet

You can also use a food processor instead of the blender to puree the fruit. Just process half of the undrained fruit and lemon juice at a time.

1   **12-ounce can (1½ cups) evaporated milk**
1   **3-ounce package orange-flavored gelatin**
1   **29- *or* 30-ounce can unpeeled apricot halves *or* peach halves**
2   **tablespoons lemon juice**

In a medium saucepan stir together milk and orange-flavored gelatin. Stir over medium heat till gelatin dissolves. Cool.

Meanwhile, place *undrained* apricots or peaches in a blender container. Add lemon juice. Cover, then blend about 1 minute or till the mixture is smooth. Stir fruit mixture into gelatin mixture in saucepan; mix well. Pour mixture into a 9x9x2-inch pan. Cover and freeze about 6 hours or till almost firm.

Break frozen mixture into chunks (see photo 2, page 56). Transfer frozen mixture to a chilled large mixer bowl. Beat with an electric mixer till smooth but not melted (see photo 3, page 56). Return quickly to the cold pan. Cover and freeze 6 to 8 hours or till firm. To serve, scoop into dessert dishes. Makes 8 to 10 servings.

Spectacular Meringues

What's light as a cloud and looks like one, too? A meringue. Meringues are s-o-o-o lightweight they practically float off your plate . . . into your mouth.

Fill or stack the crispy meringues with a flavorful filling, described in the recipes that follow. Your choices range from fruit to chocolate.

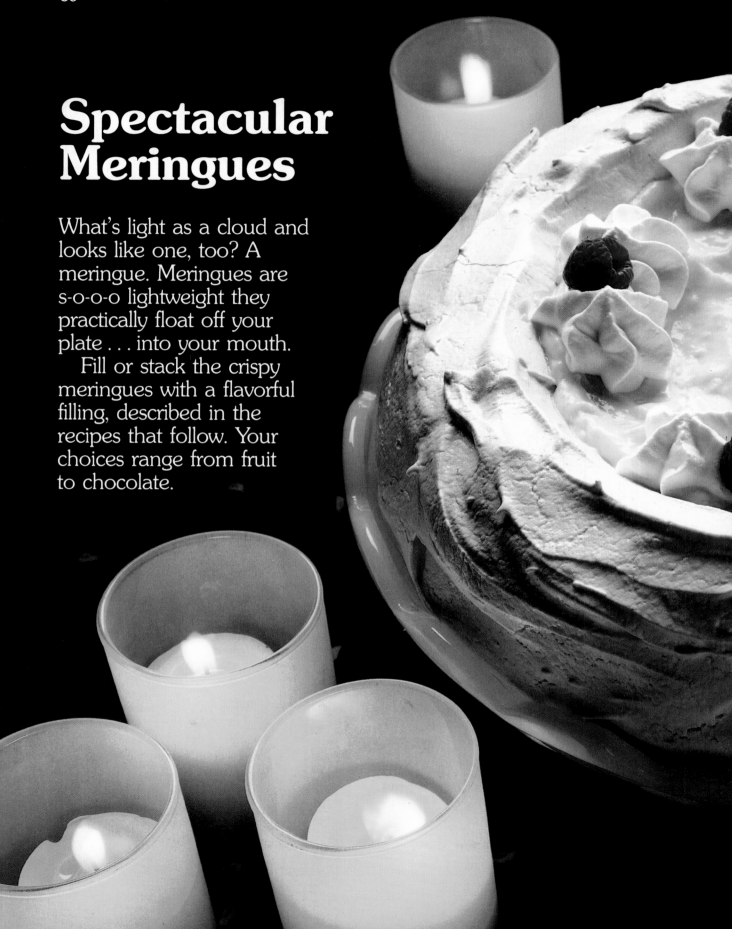

Sour Cream-Lemon Meringue Tart

Meringue Shell

3 egg whites
½ teaspoon vanilla
¼ teaspoon cream of tartar
1 cup sugar

Let egg whites stand in a small mixer bowl* about 1 hour or till they come to room temperature. Cover baking sheet with plain brown paper; draw one 9-inch circle (*see photo 1*). Add vanilla, cream of tartar, and dash *salt* to egg whites. Beat with an electric mixer on medium speed till soft peaks form (tips curl) (*see photo 2*). Add sugar, a tablespoon at a time, beating on high speed till very stiff peaks form (tips stand straight) and sugar is almost dissolved (*see photo 3*). This takes about 7 minutes.

Spread meringue over circle on paper and shape into a shell (*see photo 4*). *Or,* pipe through a pastry tube onto circle on paper, forming a shell. Bake in a 300° oven for 50 minutes. Turn off oven; let meringue dry in oven with door closed at least 1 hour (do not open oven). Peel off paper. Store in an airtight container. To serve, add filling. Makes 1 shell.

Nut Meringue Shell: Prepare Meringue Shell as above *except* fold in ½ cup finely chopped *toasted almonds* before spreading over circle.

Individual Meringue Shells: Prepare Meringue Shell as above *except* draw eight 3½-inch circles on plain brown paper. Spread or pipe meringue mixture onto circles, making 8 shells (*see tip, right*). Bake in a 300° oven for 35 minutes. Turn off oven; let shells dry in oven with door closed at least 1 hour. Makes 8.

Individual Chocolate Meringue Shells: Prepare Individual Meringue Shells as above *except* fold in ¼ cup grated *semisweet chocolate* just before spreading over eight 3½-inch circles on brown paper. Makes 8.

***Note:** For a 3-egg-white meringue, measure the mixer bowl. If small mixer bowl holds 5½ cups liquid or less, use your large mixer bowl.

1 To get an *evenly shaped* circle, trace around a baking pan, bowl, or jar lid. For a 9-inch circle, you can trace around a 9-inch round cake pan or a bowl with a top diameter of 9 inches. For individual meringues, use the lid of a mayonnaise or salad dressing jar with a 3½-inch-diameter opening.

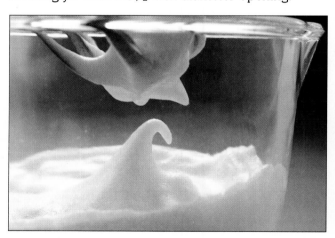

2 The eggs are easier to separate when they are cold. But remember to bring them to room temperature before beating; you'll get a greater volume. A quick trick for warming the egg whites is to set the bowl with the egg whites over a larger bowl containing a little warm water.

Beat the egg white mixture on medium speed till soft peaks form, as shown. The tips of the peaks bend over in soft curls when the beaters are lifted out, as shown.

3 Check to make sure that the sugar is almost dissolved. Rub a little of the meringue mixture between your thumb and finger, as shown. It should feel almost smooth. If the mixture feels very grainy, keep beating to further dissolve the sugar.

4 Using a spoon or spatula, spread the meringue mixture over the circle. Then shape the mixture into a shell with the back of a spoon. Make the bottom of the shell about ½ inch thick and build up the sides about 1¾ inches high.

Individual Meringues: Instead of the large meringue shell, you also can make eight individual shells from the same meringue mixture. Just draw eight 3½-inch circles on plain brown paper on a baking sheet. Pipe the mixture onto the circles, as shown, building the sides higher. *Or,* use the back of a spoon to shape the meringue mixture, as was done for the larger meringue shell.

Sour Cream-Lemon Meringue Tart

1	large Meringue Shell (see recipe, opposite)
½	cup sugar
3	tablespoon cornstarch
1⅓	cups milk
3	beaten egg yolks
½	cup dairy sour cream
2	teaspoons finely shredded lemon peel
¼	cup lemon juice
½	cup whipping cream
	Fresh raspberries

Prepare Meringue Shell (see photos 1–4). For filling, in a medium saucepan stir together sugar and cornstarch; stir in milk (see photo 1, page 50). Cook and stir over medium heat till thickened and bubbly. Reduce heat, then cook and stir 2 minutes more. Remove from heat.

Gradually stir about *half* of the hot mixture into egg yolks (see photo 2, page 50). Return to mixture in saucepan and bring to a gentle boil (see photo 3, page 51). Reduce heat. Cook and stir 2 minutes more. Remove from heat. Stir in sour cream, 2 teaspoons lemon peel, and lemon juice. Pour mixture into a bowl. Cover surface with clear plastic wrap or waxed paper (see photo 4, page 51). Cool. Chill without stirring.

Beat whipping cream (see photo 2, page 44). To assemble tart, spoon filling into Meringue Shell. Spoon or pipe whipped cream on top of the tart. If desired, garnish with raspberries. Cut into wedges. Makes 10 servings.

Double Chocolate Meringues

A perfect dessert for entertaining—most of the work is out of the way ahead of time. And serving individual meringue shells is so simple.

8 Individual Chocolate Meringue Shells
  ***or* Individual Meringue Shells**
  (see recipes, page 62)
2 egg yolks
1 tablespoon sugar
1 tablespoon crème de cacao
2 squares (2 ounces) semisweet chocolate, melted
2 egg whites
1 tablespoon sugar
1 cup whipping cream

Prepare Individual Chocolate Meringue Shells or Individual Meringue Shells (see photos 1–3 and tip, pages 62 and 63).

In a small mixer bowl beat together egg yolks and 1 tablespoon sugar till well beaten. Add crème de cacao and beat till thoroughly mixed. Fold in melted chocolate. Set aside.

Wash beaters thoroughly. In a large mixer bowl beat egg whites till soft peaks form (tips curl) (see photo 2, page 62). Gradually add 1 tablespoon sugar, beating till stiff peaks form (tips stand straight) (see photo 1, page 56). Set aside.

Beat *⅔ cup* of whipping cream (see photo 2, page 44). Fold together chocolate mixture, egg whites, and whipped cream. Chill till mixture mounds (about 1 hour).

Carefully spoon into meringue shells. Cover and chill up to 4 hours. Before serving, beat remaining whipping cream and dollop atop each serving. Makes 8 servings.

Strawberry Torte

4 egg whites
1 teaspoon vanilla
½ teaspoon cream of tartar
¼ teaspoon almond extract
¾ cup sugar
⅓ cup sliced almonds
1 cup whipping cream
2 tablespoons sugar
1 teaspoon vanilla
3 cups sliced fresh strawberries (about 4 cups whole)

Let egg whites stand in a large mixer bowl about 1 hour or till they come to room temperature. Cover 2 or 3 baking sheets with plain brown paper or foil; draw three 7-inch circles (see photo 1, page 62). Add 1 teaspoon vanilla, cream of tartar, and extract to whites. Beat with an electric mixer on medium speed till soft peaks form (tips curl) (see photo 2, page 62). Gradually add ¾ cup sugar, beating on high speed till very stiff peaks form (tips stand straight) and sugar is almost dissolved (see photo 3, page 62).

Spread *one-third* of the meringue mixture over each circle. Sprinkle each with *one-third* of the almonds. Bake in a 300° oven for 30 minutes. Turn off oven; let meringues dry in oven with door closed at least 1 hour (do not open oven).

Peel off paper from meringues. Up to 1 hour before serving, beat whipping cream, 2 tablespoons sugar, and 1 teaspoon vanilla (see photo 2, page 44). Reserve *½ cup* of whipped cream. Fold *2 cups* of strawberries into the remaining whipped cream mixture.

To assemble torte, place 1 meringue on serving plate; spread *half* of the strawberry-whipped cream mixture over it. Top with second meringue, then remaining strawberry-cream mixture. Top with third meringue. Garnish top with remaining berries and reserved whipped cream. Chill up to 1 hour before serving. Cut into wedges. Makes 8 servings.

Peach Meringue Tart

Sugar caramelizes around the almonds in the meringue shell, giving the meringue a fancy flavor.

1 **large Nut Meringue Shell (see recipe, page 62)**
5 **fresh medium peaches**
½ **cup water**
1 **teaspoon lemon juice**
¼ **cup sugar**
1 **tablespoon cornstarch**
½ **of an 8-ounce container soft-style cream cheese with pineapple**
½ **cup whipping cream**
    Sliced almonds, toasted (optional)

Prepare Nut Meringue Shell (see photos 1–4, pages 62 and 63). Peel, pit, and cut up *1* peach to make ¾ cup. In a blender container or food processor bowl, place cut-up peach, water, and lemon juice. Cover. Blend or process till pureed.

In a medium saucepan stir together ¼ cup sugar and cornstarch; stir in pureed peach mixture (see photo 1, page 50). Cook and stir till thickened and bubbly. Reduce heat, then cook and stir 2 minutes more. Remove from heat. Cover the surface with clear plastic wrap or waxed paper (see photo 4, page 51). Cool to room temperature.

Peel, pit, and slice remaining peaches. Fold into thickened mixture. To assemble tart, up to 2 hours before serving carefully spread inside of meringue shell with cheese. Spoon peach mixture over cheese layer. Cover and chill.

Just before serving, beat whipping cream (see photo 2, page 44). Dollop whipped cream on top of dessert. If desired, sprinkle a few almonds on top. Cut into wedges. Serves 8 to 10.

So-Soft Meringues

Soft meringues make fluffy dessert toppers. Bake them atop a pie. Or, poach the soft meringues in a liquid and serve them on a stirred custard or a pudding.

Pie-Top Meringues: Beat 3 *egg whites,* ½ teaspoon *vanilla,* ¼ teaspoon *cream of tartar,* and dash *salt* till soft peaks form (see photo 2, page 62). Gradually add ⅓ cup *sugar,* beating till stiff peaks form (see photo 1, page 56). Spread over hot pie filling. Seal to crust all the way around to prevent it from shrinking during baking. Bake in a 350° oven for 12 to 15 minutes. Cool.

Poached Meringues: Beat 2 *egg whites,* ½ teaspoon *vanilla,* ¼ teaspoon *cream of tartar,* and dash *salt* till soft peaks form (tips curl) (see photo 2, page 62). Gradually add ¼ cup *sugar,* beating till stiff peaks form and sugar is dissolved (tips stand straight) (see photo 1, page 56).

In a heavy 10-inch skillet heat 3 cups *milk* to simmering *(do not boil).* Drop mixture onto the milk in 6 mounds. Gently simmer, uncovered, 5 to 7 minutes. Lift from milk with a slotted spoon. Drain on paper towels. Cover and chill meringues till ready to serve. If desired, cool milk and use part of it to make a stirred custard (see recipe, page 71).

Class-Act Custards

You can turn a few simple ingredients into a sensational, people-pleasing dessert. Just bake eggs, milk, and sugar together. Your result will be a delicate custard.

Take it one step further. Toss in some extra-special ingredients and change a custard into a scrumptious bread or rice pudding.

Sound intriguing? Flip the page for proof.

Rum-Sauced Custard Ring

Rum-Sauced Custard Ring

6 **eggs**
3 **cups milk**
½ **cup sugar**
1½ **teaspoons vanilla**
½ **cup packed brown sugar**
1 **tablespoon cornstarch**
1 **to 2 tablespoons rum**
2 **tablespoons sliced almonds, toasted**

Lightly beat eggs, then stir in milk, sugar, vanilla, and ¼ teaspoon *salt* (see photo 1). Place a 4½-cup ovenproof ring mold (8-inch diameter) in a 13x9x2-inch baking pan. Place the pan on the oven rack. Pour egg mixture into the mold. Pour hot tap water into pan around mold (see photo 2). Bake in a 325° oven for 30 to 35 minutes or till done (see photo 3). Cool 1 hour; chill for 2 to 3 hours.

Meanwhile, for sauce, in a heavy saucepan stir together brown sugar and cornstarch. Stir in ⅓ cup *water*. Cook and stir till thickened and bubbly, then cook and stir 2 minutes more. Stir in rum. Cover surface with clear plastic wrap. Cool. Unmold custard (see photo 4). Garnish with almonds. Pass sauce. Makes 8 servings.

Individual Custards

For 4 custards, stir together 3 *eggs*, 1½ cups *milk,* ¼ cup *sugar,* ¾ teaspoon *vanilla,* and ⅛ teaspoon *salt* (see photo 1). Place four 6-ounce custard cups in a 9x9x2-inch baking pan. Place pan on oven rack. Pour custard mixture into cups. Pour hot tap water into pan around custard cups (see photo 2). Bake in a 350° oven 35 to 40 minutes or till done (see photo 3). Serve custards warm or chilled. Makes 4 servings.

1 Using a wire whisk or egg beater beat the eggs lightly just till whites and yolks are mixed together. Don't beat the eggs till foamy or you'll get a foamy-looking surface on the baked custard.

2 To avoid messy spills, place the mold in a baking pan and set both pans on the oven rack. Then pour custard mixture into the mold.

The next step is to pour the hottest tap water possible into the baking pan around the custard-filled mold, as shown. The water in the baking pan should be about 1 inch deep. The water bath helps distribute the heat evenly so that the custard's edges don't over-cook.

3 To test for doneness, insert a knife near the center of the baked custard. Make cut about ½ inch deep. The knife should come out clean when the custard is done. (Custards containing sour cream or yogurt may not give a completely clean knife test.) Remove from oven and water bath.

4 Loosen the edges of custard before unmolding. Carefully run a metal spatula or knife around the mold and slip the knife point down the side to let air in, as shown. Invert a plate over the custard then turn over both custard and plate together. Lift off the mold.

Tropical Bread Pudding

Coconut, orange peel, and toasted almonds make this a special-occasion version of an everyday dessert.

> **4 eggs**
> **2 cups milk**
> **¾ cup coconut**
> **½ cup sugar**
> **1 tablespoon finely shredded orange peel**
> **4 cups bread cubes (5 to 5½ slices bread)**
> **½ cup sliced almonds, toasted**

In a large mixing bowl lightly beat eggs. Stir in milk, coconut, sugar, and orange peel (see photo 1, page 68). Fold in bread cubes and almonds. Place a 10x6x2-inch baking dish in a 13x9x2-inch baking pan. Place the pan on the oven rack. Pour mixture into the 10x6x2-inch baking dish.

Pour hot tap water into the larger pan (see photo 2, page 69). Bake in a 325° oven for 40 to 45 minutes or till done (see photo 3, page 69). Serve warm. Makes 6 to 8 servings.

Peachy Rice Pudding

Old-fashioned rice pudding never tasted so good. This version, full of peaches, has a delicate orange color.

> **⅓ cup long grain rice**
> **1 16-ounce can peach slices**
> **4 eggs**
> **1 cup milk**
> **1 8-ounce carton orange yogurt**
> **½ cup sugar**
> **¼ teaspoon almond extract**
> **⅛ teaspoon salt**
> **Ground cinnamon**

Cook rice according to package directions; set aside. Drain peaches; reserve 3 slices for the garnish. Chop remaining peaches into bite-size pieces (about 1 cup).

In a large mixing bowl lightly beat eggs. Stir in milk, yogurt, sugar, almond extract, and salt (see photo 1, page 68). Stir in rice and cut-up peaches. Place a 1½-quart soufflé dish or casserole in a 13x9x2-inch baking pan. Place the pan on the oven rack. Pour mixture into the soufflé dish.

Pour hot tap water into pan around the dish (see photo 2, page 69). Bake in a 350° oven for 30 minutes. Gently stir mixture. Sprinkle with cinnamon. Bake about 25 minutes more or till set. Chill several hours. Garnish with reserved peaches. Makes 6 servings.

Baked Cottage Cheese Custard

We've kept the flavor at its fullest, but used low-fat dairy products to save calories—only 155 calories per serving of custard.

> **1¼ cups skim milk**
> **1 cup low-fat cottage cheese**
> **½ cup sugar**
> **1 teaspoon vanilla**
> **3 slightly beaten eggs**
> **Ground nutmeg**

In a blender container place milk, cottage cheese, sugar, and vanilla. Cover and blend till smooth. Add eggs. Blend on low speed just till mixed. Place six 6-ounce custard cups in a 13x9x2-inch baking pan. Place the pan on the oven rack. Divide custard mixture among the custard cups. Sprinkle with nutmeg.

Pour hot tap water into the pan around the custard cups (see photo 2, page 69). Bake in a 325° oven for 40 to 45 minutes or till done (see photo 3, page 69). Serve warm or chilled. If desired, top with fresh fruit. Makes 6 servings.

Stirred Custard

In a heavy 1½-quart saucepan use a rotary beater or wire whisk to combine 2 *eggs,* 1 cup *milk,* and 3 tablespoons *sugar.* Cook and stir the mixture over medium-low heat. Stir with a wooden spoon, frequently, using a figure-8 motion. Constant stirring ensures even cooking and keeps the mixture from burning on the bottom of the saucepan.

Continue cooking and stirring the egg mixture till it coats a metal spoon, as shown. Use a metal spoon, because the stirred custard doneness test doesn't show up as well on a wooden spoon.

To make the test, dip the spoon into the custard mixture. The excess should drip off, leaving a creamy coating slightly thicker than milk. The coating should hold its shape when you wipe a finger across the back of the spoon. Be sure to use a clean metal spoon for each test.

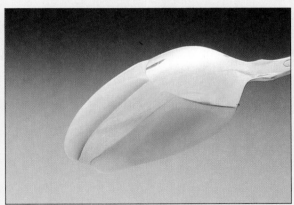

Remove saucepan from heat and immediately pour the custard into a bowl. Quickly cool the custard by placing the bowl in a larger bowl or a sink of ice water, as shown. This stops the cooking and helps prevent the custard from curdling. Stir in ½ teaspoon *vanilla or* a few drops *almond extract* and continue stirring 1 or 2 minutes to cool the mixture.

Cover surface of the custard with clear plastic wrap or waxed paper to keep a skin from forming. Chill till serving time. Serve custard over cake slices or fresh or canned fruit. Makes about 1¼ cups sauce.

Apricot Cheesecake

Luscious Cheesecakes

Go ahead and splurge!
Bake a cheesecake the
next time you crave an
outstanding dessert.

And if you're hungering
for compliments as well,
we know you'll hear
appreciative "oohs!" and
"aahs!" from others who
indulge in a wedge of your
cheesecake.

Apricot Cheesecake

¾ **cup all-purpose flour**
3 **tablespoons sugar**
2 **teaspoons finely shredded orange peel**
¼ **cup butter *or* margarine**
1 **beaten egg yolk**
1 **30-ounce can unpeeled apricot halves**
2 **8-ounce packages cream cheese,**
  softened
½ **cup sugar**
2 **tablespoons all-purpose flour**
4 **eggs**
½ **teaspoon vanilla**
3 **tablespoons orange juice**
1 **teaspoon cornstarch**
  Orange peel curls (optional)

For crust, in a mixing bowl stir together ¾ cup flour, 3 tablespoons sugar, and orange peel. Cut in butter or margarine till mixture is crumbly. Stir in egg yolk. Press *one-third* of dough onto bottom of an 8-inch springform pan (sides removed). Keep remaining dough covered. Bake crust in a 375° oven 7 minutes or till golden. Cool on a wire rack. Butter sides of the pan. Attach to the bottom. Press remaining dough 1¾ inches up sides of the pan (see photo 1).

Drain apricots, reserving ¾ cup syrup; set aside 6 apricot halves for garnish. Finely chop remaining apricots. For filling, in a large mixer bowl beat cream cheese till fluffy. Stir together ½ cup sugar and 2 tablespoons flour and add to cheese; beat till mixed. Add eggs all at once, then beat with an electric mixer on low speed about 30 seconds or just till mixed. *Do not overbeat.* Stir in ½ *cup* of reserved syrup, chopped apricots, and vanilla. Pour filling into the pastry-lined pan (see photo 2).

Bake in a 375° oven for 45 to 50 minutes or till done (see tip, page 77). Cool on a wire rack for 5 to 10 minutes. Loosen sides of cheesecake (see photo 3). Cool 30 minutes more. Remove sides of pan.

For glaze, in a small saucepan combine remaining ¼ *cup* reserved syrup, orange juice, and cornstarch. Cook and stir till thickened and bubbly, then cook and stir 2 minutes more. Remove from heat. Cover surface of glaze with waxed paper or clear plastic wrap. Cool glaze for 15 minutes. Cut reserved apricot halves in half and arrange around edge of cheesecake. Spoon glaze over apricots and cheesecake (see photo 4). Cover and chill 4 to 24 hours. If desired, garnish with orange peel curls. Serves 12.

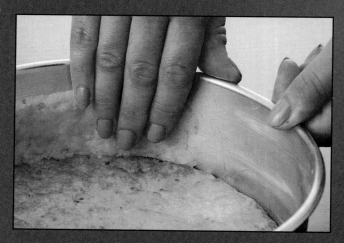

1 Press the crust mixture up the sides of the springform pan so that it sticks to the side of the pan. Use a ruler to measure the height of the crust specified in the recipe.

When cheesecake uses a crumb crust, place the springform pan in a shallow baking pan. This protects your oven in case any butter from the crust leaks out from a loose-fitting pan bottom.

2 Carefully pour the cheesecake filling into the crust-lined pan. If necessary, spread the filling with a rubber spatula to distribute the mixture evenly.

3 Cool the cheesecake 5 to 10 minutes. Then, using a metal spatula, loosen the sides from the pan. This helps keep the cheesecake edges from cracking. Cool cheesecakes with crusts 30 minutes more before removing the sides of the pan. Sometimes the top cracks. That's normal.

4 After arranging the cut fruit pieces on top of the cheesecake, spoon the thickened glaze over both fruit and cheesecake. Cover carefully, then chill the cheesecake thoroughly before serving.

Cottage Cheese Cheesecake

Sliced kiwi fruit makes an especially attractive cheese-cake garnish. Or, choose other fruit trims. Berries, peaches, and nectarines are other colorful suggestions.

1½ **cups finely crushed graham crackers**
⅓ **cup butter *or* margarine, melted**
¼ **cup sugar**
1 **cup cream-style cottage cheese**
2 **8-ounce packages cream cheese, softened**
¾ **cup sugar**
2 **tablespoons all-purpose flour**
2 **teaspoons vanilla**
3 **eggs**
¼ **cup light cream *or* milk**
1 **8-ounce carton dairy sour cream**
1 **cup sliced fresh fruit**

For crust, in a mixing bowl stir together crushed graham crackers, butter or margarine, and ¼ cup sugar. Press mixture evenly over the bottom and 1¾ inches up sides of a 9-inch springform pan (see photo 1, page 74). Place the pan in a shallow baking pan.

For filling, in a large mixer bowl beat *undrained* cottage cheese till almost smooth. Beat in cream cheese, ¾ cup sugar, flour, and vanilla. Add eggs all at once, then beat with an electric mixer on low speed just till mixed. *Do not over-beat.* Stir in cream or milk. Pour filling into the crumb-lined pan (see photo 2, page 75).

Bake in a 350° oven for 50 to 60 minutes or till done (see tip, page 77). Cool on a wire rack for 5 to 10 minutes. Loosen sides of cheesecake (see photo 3, page 75). Spread sour cream over top. Cool 30 minutes more. Remove sides of pan. Cover and chill 4 to 24 hours. To serve, arrange fruit atop cheesecake. Serves 12 to 14.

Individual Pumpkin Cheesecakes

1 **cup finely crushed zwieback**
3 **tablespoons sugar**
3 **tablespoons butter *or* margarine, melted**
1 **8-ounce package cream cheese, softened**
¾ **cup canned pumpkin**
⅓ **cup sugar**
1 **teaspoon pumpkin pie spice**
½ **teaspoon vanilla**
⅛ **teaspoon salt**
2 **eggs**
½ **cup light cream *or* milk**
½ **cup whipping cream**

For crust, in a mixing bowl stir together crushed zwieback, 3 tablespoons sugar, and butter or margarine. Divide crumb mixture evenly among eight 6-ounce custard cups. Press onto the bottom and ¾ of the way up sides of cups to form a firm, even crust (see photo 1, page 74).

For filling, in a small mixer bowl beat together cream cheese, pumpkin, ⅓ cup sugar, pumpkin pie spice, vanilla, and salt till combined. Add eggs all at once, then beat with an electric mixer on low speed just till mixed. *Do not overbeat.* Stir in light cream or milk. Pour filling into prepared custard cups (see photo 2, page 75). Place custard cups in a shallow baking pan.

Bake in a 375° oven for 20 to 25 minutes or till done (see tip, page 77). Cool for 15 minutes. Cover and chill 2 to 24 hours. Loosen sides of cheesecakes from cups with a spatula; remove from custard cups. Place each cheesecake in an individual serving dish. Beat whipping cream (see photo 2, page 44). Dollop each cheesecake with whipped cream. Makes 8 servings.

Poppy Seed Cheesecake

The cake and pastry filling used for the topper is different from canned pie filling. Be sure to check the label.

1 **cup all-purpose flour**
¼ **cup sugar**
¼ **cup butter *or* margarine**
2 **beaten egg yolks**
3 **8-ounce packages cream cheese, softened**
1 **cup sugar**
1 **teaspoon vanilla**
4 **eggs**
1 **12½-ounce can poppy seed *or* cherry cake and pastry filling**
1 **tablespoon lemon juice**
¼ **cup quick-cooking rolled oats**
¼ **cup all-purpose flour**
2 **tablespoons brown sugar**
2 **tablespoons butter *or* margarine**

For crust, in a mixing bowl combine 1 cup flour and ¼ cup sugar. Cut in ¼ cup butter or margarine till crumbly. Combine yolks and 1 tablespoon *water;* stir into flour mixture. Press *one-third* dough onto bottom of an 8- or 9-inch springform pan (sides removed). Bake in a 375° oven 7 minutes or till golden. Cool on a wire rack. Butter sides of pan. Attach to the bottom. Press remaining dough 1½ inches up sides of the pan for a 9-inch pan and 2 inches up sides for an 8-inch pan (see photo 1, page 74).

For filling, in a large mixer bowl beat cream cheese till fluffy. Add sugar and vanilla. Beat till mixed. Add eggs all at once, then beat with an electric mixer on low speed just till mixed. *Do not overbeat.* Pour into the pastry-lined pan (see photo 2, page 75).

Bake in a 375° oven till done (see tip, right). Bake 40 to 45 minutes for the 9-inch pan and 45 to 50 minutes for the 8-inch pan. Cool on a wire rack for 5 minutes. Increase the oven temperature to 450°.

Meanwhile, combine poppy seed or cherry filling and lemon juice. Carefully spread mixture over hot baked cheesecake. For topping, stir together oats, ¼ cup flour, and brown sugar. Cut in 2 tablespoons butter or margarine till mixture resembles coarse crumbs (see photo 1, page 12). Sprinkle over filling.

Bake in a 450° oven for 10 to 15 minutes more or till topping is lightly brown. Cool on a wire rack for 5 to 10 minutes. Loosen sides of cheesecake (see photo 3, page 75). Cool 30 minutes more. Remove sides of pan. Cover and chill 4 to 24 hours. Makes 12 to 14 servings.

How Do You Know Your Cheesecake Is Done?

To test your cheesecake for doneness, gently shake the side of the pan. The center should appear *nearly* set. Frequently a 1-inch portion in the center of the baked dessert will jiggle slightly at the end of the baking time when the cheesecake is done.

Another doneness test is to insert a knife halfway between the center and the edge of the cheesecake. If the knife comes out clean, the cheesecake is done. A crack may form in cheesecake where the knife was inserted.

The knife test may not give an accurate doneness test for cheesecakes containing sour cream. To test these cheesecakes, gently shake the pan. A slightly larger portion in the center will seem unset but will firm after cooling the cheesecake.

Calorie-Trimmed Cheesecake

Want to save even more calories than this 198-calories-per-serving cheesecake offers? Cut the cheesecake into 14 wedges instead of 12—that's 170 calories per cheesecake wedge.

½ **cup finely crushed graham crackers**
4 **teaspoons butter *or* margarine, melted**
1 **cup part-skim ricotta cheese**
12 **ounces Neufchâtel cheese, softened**
¾ **cup sugar**
2 **tablespoons all-purpose flour**
1 **teaspoon vanilla**
2 **eggs**
¼ **cup skim milk**
1 **cup sliced fresh strawberries**

For crust, in a mixing bowl stir together crushed graham crackers and butter or margarine. Press mixture evenly over the bottom only of an 8-inch springform pan. Place the pan in a shallow baking pan.

For filling, in a large mixer bowl beat ricotta cheese with an electric mixer till almost smooth. Add Neufchâtel cheese, sugar, flour, and vanilla and beat till well mixed. Add eggs all at once, then beat on low speed just till mixed. *Do not overbeat.* Stir in milk. Pour filling into the crumb-lined pan (see photo 2, page 75).

Bake in a 375° oven for 30 to 35 minutes or till done (see tip, page 77). Cool on a wire rack for 5 to 10 minutes. Loosen sides of cheesecake (see photo 3, page 75). Remove sides of pan. Cover and chill 4 to 24 hours. To serve, arrange strawberries atop cheesecake. Serves 12 to 14.

Triple Chocolate Cheesecake

Truly a chocolate lover's dream come true. You'll find chocolate in three places: the crust, the filling, and even in the drizzled-on topping.

1½ **cups finely crushed chocolate wafers**
⅓ **cup butter *or* margarine, melted**
3 **8-ounce packages cream cheese, softened**
1½ **cups sugar**
4 **squares (4 ounces) semisweet chocolate, melted and cooled**
2 **tablespoons all-purpose flour**
1 **teaspoon vanilla**
4 **eggs**
¼ **cup milk**
1 **square (1 ounce) semisweet chocolate**
2 **teaspoons shortening**

For crust, in a mixing bowl stir together crushed wafers and butter or margarine. Press mixture evenly over the bottom and 1¾ inches up sides of a 9-inch springform pan (see photo 1, page 74). Place the pan in a shallow baking pan.

For filling, in a large mixer bowl beat cream cheese, sugar, 4 squares melted chocolate, flour, and vanilla till well mixed. Add eggs all at once, then beat with an electric mixer on low speed just till mixed. *Do not overbeat.* Stir in milk. Pour filling into the crumb-lined pan (see photo 2, page 75).

Bake in a 350° oven about 45 minutes or till done (see tip, page 77). Cool on a wire rack 5 to 10 minutes. Loosen sides of cheesecake (see photo 3, page 75). Cool 30 minutes. Remove sides of pan. Cover and chill 4 to 24 hours.

For topping, in a small saucepan melt 1 square chocolate and shortening over low heat. Drizzle in lattice design atop chilled cheesecake. Chill till topping is set. Makes 12 to 14 servings.

◀ *Pictured opposite: Triple Chocolate Cheesecake*

Shapely Crepes

All crepes start off round and flat, like very thin pancakes. From there you choose the shape. Roll them . . . fold them . . . or form them into cups.

However you shape them, we can promise that your dessert crepes will be filled with fun as well as lots of flavor.

Strawberry-Pineapple
Crepe Cup Flambé

Dessert Crepes

1½ cups milk
1 cup all-purpose flour
2 eggs
2 tablespoons sugar
1 tablespoon cooking oil
⅛ teaspoon salt

In a mixing bowl combine milk, flour, eggs, sugar, cooking oil, and salt. Beat with a rotary beater till mixed. Lightly grease a 6-inch skillet or crepe pan (see photo 1). Heat skillet till a drop of water sizzles. Remove from heat. Spoon *2 tablespoons* batter into skillet (see photo 2). Lift and tilt skillet to spread batter. Return to heat.

When crepe is lightly browned on bottom, invert pan over paper towels and remove crepe. (*Or,* cook on inverted crepe pan following manufacturer's directions). Repeat with remaining batter to make 16 to 18 crepes. Grease skillet occasionally. Cool crepes completely. To freeze crepes, stack with 2 layers of waxed paper between crepes (see photo 3).

Dessert Crepe Cups: Prepare and cook Dessert Crepes as above. In a shallow baking pan shape over greased custard cups (see photo 4). Bake in a 350° oven for 20 to 22 minutes or till crepes are crisp on edges and hold their shape. Remove from custard cups. Place dessert cups, browned side down, in the baking pan. Return to oven for 3 to 5 minutes or till crisp.

Nutty Dessert Crepes: Prepare the Dessert Crepes as above, *except* reduce flour to *¾ cup* and stir in ¼ cup very finely chopped *pecans.* Continue as directed.

Calorie Counter's Crepes: Prepare Dessert Crepes as above, *except* use *skim milk.* Substitute 1 *egg* and 1 *egg white* for the 2 eggs; omit sugar and cooking oil. Continue as directed.

1 Use a pastry brush to lightly grease a 6-inch skillet or crepe pan with shortening or cooking oil, as shown. Grease pan occasionally between crepes. Avoid using brushes with nylon bristles since the bristles can melt.

For best results, use a pan with sloping sides instead of a straight-sided pan to make crepes.

2 For handy pouring, use a ⅛-cup coffee measure or half of a ¼-cup measure. Lift the crepe pan off the heat when you add the batter, as shown. Quickly tilt the pan round and round to evenly spread the batter before it starts to cook. For each crepe, use *2 tablespoons* of the batter.

3 Save some time and make your crepes days or even weeks before serving them. Crepes freeze well to use later.

To freeze crepes, stack them with two sheets of waxed paper between crepes. That way they'll be easier to separate. Place the stack in a freezer container or in a moisture-vaporproof freezer bag. Seal, label, and freeze the crepes up to four months. Let the crepes thaw at room temperature about an hour before using them.

4 To make crepe cups, generously grease the outside of 6-ounce custard cups. Invert custard cups in a large shallow baking pan or on a cookie sheet. Place a crepe, browned side up, atop each custard cup and lightly press to fit, as shown.

Repeat shaping the desired number of crepe cups, then bake. After baking, remove the crepes from cups. Return the shaped crepes to the oven and bake 3 to 5 minutes more to crisp.

Strawberry-Pineapple Crepe Cup Flambé

8	Dessert Crepe Cups (see recipe, left)
1	8-ounce can pineapple tidbits (juice pack)
1	quart strawberries
¼	cup sugar
2	tablespoons cornstarch
	Few drops red food coloring (optional)
3	tablespoons orange liqueur

Prepare Dessert Crepe Cups (see photos 1, 2, and 4). For filling, drain pineapple, reserving juice. Set pineapple aside. Add water to juice to measure 1 cup liquid. In a small saucepan crush *1 cup* of strawberries. Stir in reserved liquid. Bring to boiling. Reduce heat, then simmer, uncovered, for 2 minutes. Strain mixture through a cheesecloth-lined sieve (should have 1¼ cups liquid). Slice remaining strawberries. Set aside.

In a small saucepan combine sugar and cornstarch. Stir in sieved berry mixture. Cook and stir over medium heat till thickened and bubbly, then cook and stir 2 minutes more. Stir in drained pineapple and food coloring, if desired.

To assemble, divide sliced strawberries evenly among crepe cups. Spoon hot pineapple mixture over berries. In a small saucepan heat the liqueur just till warm. Carefully ignite with a long match (see photo 5). Ladle flaming liqueur over filling in each cup. Serve the filled crepe cups immediately. Makes 8 servings.

5 When flaming a dessert, use a liqueur that is at least 70 proof to get a flame. Pour the liqueur into a small saucepan and heat over low heat or over the flame of a candle just till warm. Using a long match, ignite the liqueur, as shown.

Nutty Crème Crepes

Want to serve these tonight? Top the filled crepes with some whipped cream or dairy sour cream, instead of the Crème Fraîche.

¼ to ½ cup Crème Fraîche
8 Nutty Dessert Crepes (see recipe, page 82)
¼ cup red raspberry preserves
¼ cup sliced almonds, toasted

Prepare Crème Fraîche. Chill in the refrigerator. Prepare Nutty Dessert Crepes (see photos 1–2, page 82).

To assemble, spread unbrowned side of each crepe with about *½ tablespoon* raspberry preserves. Fold crepe in half, then in half again, forming a triangle. Place 2 filled crepes on each serving plate. Drizzle with the Crème Fraîche. Sprinkle with nuts. Makes 4 servings.

Crème Fraîche: In a small saucepan heat 1 cup *whipping cream* to between 90° and 100°F. Pour into a small bowl. Stir in ¼ cup *buttermilk*. Cover and let stand at room temperature for 18 to 24 hours or till mixture is thickened, stirring occasionally. Store in a covered container in the refrigerator for up to 1 week. Makes 1¼ cups.

Apricot Crepes

8 Dessert Crepes (see recipe, page 82)
1 16-ounce can unpeeled apricot halves
¾ cup ricotta cheese
¼ teaspoon vanilla
1 tablespoon cornstarch
¼ teaspoon ground nutmeg
1 tablespoon lemon juice
1 tablespoon butter *or* margarine

Prepare Dessert Crepes (see photos 1–2, page 82). Drain apricots, reserving syrup. In a small mixer bowl beat *1 tablespoon* of the reserved syrup, ricotta cheese, and vanilla with an electric mixer on medium speed till creamy. Chop *6* of the apricot halves. Stir the chopped apricots into ricotta mixture.

To assemble, spoon *one-eighth* of cheese mixture over unbrowned side of each crepe to within ¼ inch of the edge. Fold in half, then fold in half again, forming a triangle. Repeat with the remaining crepes.

For sauce, add enough water to the remaining reserved syrup to make *1 cup* liquid. In a 10-inch skillet or chafing dish combine syrup mixture, cornstarch, and nutmeg. Cook and stir the mixture till thickened and bubbly, then cook and stir 2 minutes more. Stir in lemon juice and butter or margarine till melted.

Arrange crepes and remaining apricot halves in sauce in skillet. Heat through. Serve filled crepes warm. Makes 4 servings.

Chocolate Coconut-Cream Crepes

8 **Dessert Crepes (see recipe, page 82)**
¼ **cup sugar**
1 **tablespoon cornstarch**
¾ **cup milk**
1 **square (1 ounce) semisweet chocolate, cut up**
1 **tablespoon butter *or* margarine**
¼ **cup coconut, toasted**
  Powdered sugar
  Strawberries, halved

Prepare Dessert Crepes (see photos 1–2, page 82). In a saucepan combine sugar and cornstarch. Stir in milk. Cook and stir till bubbly, then cook 2 minutes more. Stir in chocolate and butter till melted. Remove from heat. Cover surface with clear plastic wrap. Chill 3 hours.

Fold coconut into chocolate mixture. Spoon some down center of unbrowned side of each crepe. Fold opposite edges of crepe to overlap atop filling. Place 2 crepes on each plate. Top with powdered sugar and berries. Serves 4.

Calorie-Cutting Cantaloupe Crepes

Here's a fresh-tasting dessert that boasts a slim 200 calories for each serving.

8 **Calorie Counter's Crepes (see recipe, page 82)**
½ **medium cantaloupe**
⅓ **of a 4-ounce carton (about ½ cup) frozen whipped dessert topping, thawed**
½ **cup lemon yogurt**
1 **tablespoon broken pecans**

Prepare Calorie Counter's Crepes (see photos 1–2, page 82). Cut cantaloupe into 8 small slices. Remove peel from slices. In a mixing bowl fold whipped topping into yogurt.

Spread about *1 tablespoon* of the yogurt mixture on unbrowned side of each crepe. Place 1 melon slice in center of each crepe. Roll up jelly-roll style. Place 2 filled crepes, seam side down, on each dessert plate. Dollop remaining yogurt mixture on top. Sprinkle nuts on top. Serves 4.

Crepe Shaping

Roll 'em, fold 'em, or overlap 'em. These are different ways to shape a crepe.

To fold crepes, spread the filling over the unbrowned side of each crepe. Fold the crepe in half, then fold in half again, forming a triangle, as shown, left.

For overlapped crepes, spoon the filling along the center of the unbrowned side of each crepe. Fold the two opposite edges so that they overlap on top of the filling, as shown, center. Place them either folded edges up or down on the dessert plate.

As the name implies, to roll up crepes, simply spread with a filling, then roll up like a jelly roll, as shown, right.

Puff Pastry Panache

Who would guess that the formula for such a spectacular-looking dessert is so simple? The secret is to start with purchased frozen puff pastry.

For this creation, shape and bake some puff pastry dough. Add a luscious coconut filling. Then, top it off with ice cream topping.

The delicious results will prove to you that minimum effort can yield a maximum taste.

Coconut Tart

Coconut Tart

Use small hors d'oeuvre cutters to cut the pastry scraps into decorations, or cut them freehand. Bake cutouts on a baking sheet for 12 to 15 minutes, then cool.

½	**cup sugar**
3	**tablespoons cornstarch**
1⅓	**cups milk**
2	**beaten egg yolks**
¼	**cup toasted coconut**
2	**tablespoons coconut liqueur *or* white crème de cacao**
½	**of a 17½-ounce package (1 sheet) frozen puff pastry**
⅓	**cup fudge ice cream topping**

For filling, in a small saucepan combine sugar and cornstarch. Stir in milk (see photo 1, page 50). Cook and stir over medium heat till thickened and bubbly, then cook 2 minutes more. Remove from heat. Stir about *1 cup* hot mixture into egg yolks (see photo 2, page 50). Return to mixture in saucepan. Bring just to a boil. Cook and stir 2 minutes more. Remove from heat. Stir in coconut and liqueur. Cover surface with clear plastic wrap (see photo 4, page 51). Chill, without stirring, about 6 hours or till cold.

Thaw pastry according to package directions. On a lightly floured surface lightly roll pastry sheet into a 10-inch square (see photo 1). Cut four 1-inch strips off of one side, making a 10x6-inch rectangle (see photo 2). Transfer pastry rectangle to an ungreased baking sheet. Prick pastry rectangle at 1-inch intervals, making definite holes in pastry so you can see the pan through the holes. Trim *2* of the strips to 6-inch lengths. Gently twist all strips. Place on the edges of the pastry rectangle to form a rim around edge (see photo 3). Moisten ends. Press together lightly to adhere.

Bake in a 375° oven about 25 minutes or till pastry is golden brown. Carefully loosen and remove pastry from pan. Cool on a wire rack.

To serve, place pastry on a serving platter. Heat fudge topping till warm. Reserve *1 tablespoon* topping. Spread remaining topping in bottom of pastry. Beat filling till smooth. Spoon dollops of filling over fudge topping in pastry rectangle. Spread evenly to rim. Drizzle reserved topping over top (see photo 4). If desired, garnish with pastry cutouts. Slice to serve. Makes 6 servings.

1 Lightly flour the work surface. Use a lightly floured rolling pin to roll the thawed puff pastry sheet into a 10-inch square. Measure the pastry square with a ruler to check the dimensions before you begin trimming off strips.

4 Drizzle topping over the filling using a back and forth pattern, as shown. Then, run a knife through the topping from one end of pastry to the other. Make 4 or 5 "cuts" to give the webbed design.

2 Cut off four 1-inch strips from one side of the pastry square, as shown. Press straight down with a chef's knife for a clean cut—don't drag the knife or the pastry won't puff nicely along edges. This leaves a 10x6-inch rectangle.

3 Gently twist the pastry strips and place them on the edges of the pastry rectangle. Moisten the ends of the strips with water and press till they stick together. The pastry strips form a rim for the filling.

Piecrust Creations

Turn a simple pastry into a medley of terrific desserts.

From the single-crust recipe, make a flaky pie shell for a luscious filling. Or, cut the pastry into strips or squares, then wrap the pastry around fruit for dumplings or turnovers.

Give the double-crust pastry a try, too! Bake a double-delicious fruit pie such as Ginger Peachy Pie, at right.

Ginger Peachy Pie

Single-Crust Pastry

1¼ **cups all-purpose flour**
¼ **teaspoon salt**
⅓ **cup shortening *or* lard**
3 **to 4 tablespoons cold water**

In a mixing bowl stir together flour and salt. Cut in shortening or lard till pieces are the size of small peas (see photo 1). Sprinkle *1 tablespoon* water over part of mixture, gently tossing with a fork. Push to side of the bowl. Repeat with water till all is moistened. Form dough into a ball.

On a lightly floured surface flatten dough with hands (see photo 2). Roll dough into a 12-inch circle (see photo 3). Ease pastry into a 9-inch pie plate (do not stretch).

Trim pastry to ½ inch beyond edge of pie plate. Fold under extra pastry and flute edge. Prick bottom and sides with tines of a fork. Bake in a 450° oven for 10 to 12 minutes or till golden.

Double-Crust Pastry: Prepare Single-Crust Pastry as above, *except* use *2 cups* all-purpose flour, *½ teaspoon* salt, *⅔ cup* shortening or lard, and *6 to 7 tablespoons* cold water. Divide dough in half. Form dough into 2 balls. Roll out 1 ball as above and fit into pie plate. Trim pastry even with edge of pie plate. For top crust, roll out remaining dough and cut slits for steam to escape (see photo 4). Add desired filling to pastry in pie plate. Add the top crust. Trim top crust ½ inch beyond edge of pie plate. Fold extra pastry under bottom crust and flute edge. Bake as directed in pie recipe.

1 Use a pastry blender (or two knives, cutting with a crossing motion) to cut in the shortening till the pieces are the size of small peas, as shown. Don't overdo it by cutting in the shortening too much or the pastry won't be light and flaky.

2 Lightly flour your work surface for rolling out the pastry. Or, use a floured pastry cloth for rolling.

Flatten the ball of dough with your hands, as shown. Smooth the edges, keeping pastry in a circle.

3 Using a floured rolling pin or one with a floured cover, roll out the pastry. Roll from the center to the edge with light, even strokes until the pastry circle measures 12 inches in diameter. Use as little flour as possible when rolling the pastry. Too much flour causes pastry to become tough.

4 For a two-crust pie, cut slits in the top crust to let the steam escape during baking. This keeps the underside of the top crust from becoming soggy and prevents steam pressure from tearing the crust. Make cuts after rolling out the top crust, as shown. Use a knife to cut decorative designs in the top crust or use small hors d'oeuvre or cookie cutters for pastry cutouts. Prick the top crust of the turnovers, too.

5 Prevent a too-brown edge on a double-crust pie by covering it with foil during part of the baking. To make the foil rim, fold a 12-inch square of foil into quarters. Cut out the center portion, making a 7½-inch circle. Unfold and loosely mold the foil rim over the edge of the pie, as shown.

Ginger Peachy Pie

½	cup packed brown sugar
¼	cup sugar
3	tablespoons all-purpose flour
5	cups sliced peeled peaches (2 to 2½ pounds) *or* 5 cups frozen unsweetened peach slices* (20 ounces)
2	teaspoons lemon juice
4	teaspoons finely chopped crystallized ginger *or* ¼ teaspoon ground ginger
	Double-Crust Pastry (see recipe, left)
1	tablespoon butter *or* margarine
	Milk
	Sugar

In a mixing bowl stir together brown sugar, ¼ cup sugar, and flour. Sprinkle fresh or thawed peaches with lemon juice. Add peaches and crystallized or ground ginger to sugar mixture. Toss till thoroughly combined. Let the mixture stand 15 minutes.

Meanwhile, prepare and roll out Double-Crust Pastry and line a 9-inch pie plate (see photos 1–3). Transfer peach mixture to pastry-lined pie plate. Dot with butter or margarine. Add top crust which has slits cut (see photo 4). Trim pastry, fold extra pastry under bottom crust, and flute edge. Brush top crust with milk, then sprinkle with sugar.

To prevent overbrowning, cover edge of pie with foil (see photo 5). Bake in a 375° oven for 25 minutes. Remove foil and bake for 25 to 30 minutes more or till crust is golden. Cool. Makes 8 servings.

***Note:** If using frozen peaches, measure peaches while frozen and pour into a mixing bowl. Cover and let thaw. Do not drain off the liquid before mixing with other ingredients.

Java Cream Pie

A wonderfully rich pie, with a flavor reminiscent of coffee with cream.

Single-Crust Pastry (see recipe, page 92)
¾ cup sugar
3 tablespoons cornstarch
2 teaspoons instant coffee crystals
2 cups milk
2 eggs
½ of a 6-ounce package (½ cup) semisweet chocolate pieces
2 tablespoons butter *or* margarine
½ teaspoon vanilla
½ cup whipping cream, whipped
Chocolate curls

Prepare and roll out Single-Crust Pastry and line a 9-inch pie plate (see photos 1–3, page 92). Prick and bake pastry. Set aside to cool.

For filling, in a medium saucepan combine sugar, cornstarch, and coffee crystals. Stir in milk (see photo 1, page 50). Cook and stir over medium heat till mixture is thickened and bubbly, then cook and stir 2 minutes more. Remove from heat.

Gradually stir about *half* of the hot mixture into eggs (see photo 2, page 50). Return to mixture in saucepan. Cook and stir till nearly bubbly (see photo 3, page 51). Reduce heat. Cook and stir 2 minutes more. Do not boil. Remove from heat. Stir in chocolate pieces, butter or margarine, and vanilla till chocolate is melted.

Pour mixture into cooled pie shell. Cover surface with clear plastic wrap or waxed paper (see photo 4, page 51). Chill 4 hours.

Carefully remove plastic wrap or waxed paper. Pipe whipped cream over top of pie and garnish with chocolate curls. Makes 8 servings.

Summer Fruit Tart

1¾ cups all-purpose flour
½ teaspoon salt
½ cup shortening
4 to 5 tablespoons cold water
3 tablespoons sugar
1 tablespoon cornstarch
1 cup unsweetened pineapple juice
2 5-ounce jars cream cheese spread with pineapple
¾ cup sifted powdered sugar
⅓ cup finely chopped pecans
3 cups of desired fruits
   (halved strawberries, blueberries, pineapple tidbits, sliced bananas, sliced peaches, *or* halved grapes)

For crust, in a mixing bowl stir together flour and salt. Cut in shortening till pieces are the size of small peas (see photo 1, page 92). Sprinkle *1 tablespoon* water over part of mixture, gently tossing with a fork. Push to the side of the bowl. Repeat with remaining water till all is moistened. Form dough into a ball. On a lightly floured surface flatten dough with hands (see photo 2, page 92). Roll dough from center to edge, forming a 15-inch circle.

Fold pastry into quarters and transfer to a 12-inch pizza pan. Unfold and ease into pan. Trim pastry to ½ inch beyond edge of pan. Fold under extra pastry and flute edge. Prick pastry with tines of a fork. Bake in a 425° oven for 12 to 15 minutes or till golden. Cool.

Meanwhile, for glaze, in a saucepan stir together sugar and cornstarch. Stir in pineapple juice. Cook and stir till mixture is thickened and bubbly, then cook and stir 2 minutes more. Cover surface of mixture with clear plastic wrap or waxed paper (see photo 4, page 51). Cool.

In a mixing bowl combine cream cheese, powdered sugar, and nuts. Beat till mixed. To assemble tart, spread cheese mixture over cooled pastry. Arrange desired fruit over cheese. Carefully spoon cooled pineapple glaze over fruit to cover. Chill up to 2 hours. Makes 10 servings.

Apple-Berry Turnovers

Seal the pastry well to help prevent the filling from leaking out during baking.

Single-Crust Pastry (see recipe, page 92)
¼ **cup sugar**
1 **tablespoon all-purpose flour**
½ **teaspoon finely shredded orange peel**
⅛ **teaspoon ground cinnamon**
1 **cup fresh *or* frozen blueberries**
1 **medium cooking apple, peeled, cored, and coarsely chopped**
   Milk
   Sugar

Prepare Single-Crust pastry (see photo 1, page 92). On a lightly floured surface roll out pastry into a 15x10-inch rectangle (see photos 2–3, page 92). Cut into six 5-inch squares. Cover with clear plastic wrap while preparing filling.

For filling, in a mixing bowl combine ¼ cup sugar, flour, orange peel, and cinnamon. Fold in blueberries and apple.

Spoon about ⅓ cup of the filling onto each pastry square. Moisten edges of pastry with a little water. Fold each pastry square in half diagonally, sealing edges well by pressing with tines of fork. Place on an ungreased baking sheet. Prick tops. Brush lightly with milk and sprinkle with sugar. Bake in a 375° oven about 30 minutes or till golden. Serve the turnovers warm or cool. Makes 6 servings.

Wrapped Pear Dumplings

A beautiful presentation for a mouth-watering dessert.

Single-Crust Pastry (see recipe, page 92)
¼ **cup apricot preserves**
2 **tablespoons chopped walnuts**
4 **small pears, peeled and cored**
1 **tablespoon butter *or* margarine, melted**
   Ground cinnamon
⅔ **cup water**
¼ **cup sugar**
2 **tablespoons brown sugar**
2 **tablespoons butter *or* margarine**
½ **teaspoon vanilla**
   Light cream *or* vanilla ice cream (optional)

Prepare Single-Crust Pastry (see photo 1, page 92). On a lightly floured surface roll out the pastry into a 14x8-inch rectangle (see photos 2–3, page 92). Cut into eight 14x1-inch strips. Set the strips aside.

In a mixing bowl combine preserves and walnuts. Fill center of each pear with some of the preserves mixture. Using *1* of the pastry strips and starting at base of pear, wrap pastry strip around pear, overlapping edges of strip to enclose bottom half of pear. Moisten end and seal to end of second pastry strip. Complete wrapping pear with pastry.

With a spatula, transfer pear to an 8x8x2-inch baking dish. Repeat with remaining pears and pastry. Brush with 1 tablespoon melted butter or margarine and sprinkle with cinnamon.

In a saucepan combine water, sugar, and brown sugar. Cook and stir over medium heat till sugar is dissolved. Stir in 2 tablespoons butter or margarine and vanilla. Pour around dumplings in baking dish. Bake in a 400° oven for 35 to 40 minutes or till dumplings are golden. Serve with cream or ice cream, if desired. Makes 4 servings.

Choice Cream Puffs

Remember the childhood story "The Ugly Duckling" and how something so unpromising turned into something so beautiful?

Cream puffs are the ugly ducklings of pastry desserts. You'll be delighted at how a homely glob of dough blossoms into a handsome cream puff as you bake it.

Orange-Filled Cream Puffs

Cream Puffs

1	**cup water**
½	**cup butter *or* margarine**
1	**cup all-purpose flour**
¼	**teaspoon salt**
4	**eggs**

In a medium saucepan combine water and butter or margarine. Bring to boiling, stirring till butter or margarine melts. Add flour and salt all at once, stirring vigorously. Cook and stir till mixture forms a ball that doesn't separate (see photo 1). Remove from heat and cool 10 minutes. Add eggs, 1 at a time, beating with a wooden spoon after each addition till mixture is smooth (see photo 2).

Drop batter by heaping tablespoons into 10 mounds, 3 inches apart, onto a greased baking sheet (see photo 3). Bake in a 400° oven about 35 minutes or till golden brown and puffy. Remove from oven. Cut off tops and remove any soft dough inside (see photo 4). Cool on a wire rack. Makes 10 cream puffs.

Note: Freeze any leftover cream puffs in a tightly covered container for up to 2 months.

Orange-Filled Cream Puffs

6	**Cream Puffs (see recipe, left)**
¾	**cup sugar**
3	**tablespoons cornstarch**
1½	**cups orange juice**
3	**beaten egg yolks**
1	**8-ounce carton plain yogurt**
2	**tablespoons butter *or* margarine**
1	**11-ounce can mandarin orange sections, drained**
	Powdered sugar

Prepare Cream Puffs (see photos 1–4). For filling, in a medium saucepan combine sugar and cornstarch. Stir in orange juice (see photo 1, page 50). Cook and stir over medium heat till thickened and bubbly, then cook and stir 2 minutes more. Remove from heat. Gradually stir *half* of hot mixture into egg yolks (see photo 2, page 50). Return to mixture in saucepan. Bring to a gentle boil (see photo 3, page 51). Cook and stir 2 minutes more. Remove from heat. Stir in yogurt and butter. Pour mixture into a bowl. Cover surface with clear plastic wrap (see photo 4, page 51). Chill 4 hours.

To serve, spoon filling into bottoms of cream puffs (see photo 5). Pile orange sections atop filling. Add cream puff tops. Lightly sift powdered sugar over tops. Makes 6 servings.

1 Use a wooden spoon to stir the flour and salt into the butter-water mixture while it's over the heat. Continue cooking and stirring over medium heat till the mixture forms a smooth ball of dough that doesn't separate, as shown.

2 Remove the saucepan from the heat. Let the flour mixture cool slightly so when you add the eggs they don't cook before they're mixed in.

Add the eggs, one at a time, beating 1 to 2 minutes after each. The mixture should be thick, smooth, and slightly sticky to the touch after all eggs are added.

3 Use a tablespoon to drop the cream puff dough onto a greased baking sheet. Push the dough off the spoon with another spoon or a spatula. Drop the dough in mounded rounds for best appearance.

4 While the puffs are hot from the oven, split each with a knife and remove any soft dough inside. Use a fork to gently lift out the soft dough, as shown. This leaves a crisp, hollow puff that's ready to be cooled and filled.

5 Fill the puffs just before serving so they don't get soggy. Spoon in the filling, as shown, then add the cream puff tops. Lightly dust tops with powdered sugar, shaking the sugar through a sieve or sifter.

Slimming Pumpkin Puffs

You get three puffs per serving, but only 189 calories!

½ cup water
2 tablespoons butter *or* margarine
½ cup all-purpose flour
2 eggs
½ cup canned pumpkin
1 tablespoon brown sugar
¼ teaspoon ground ginger
⅛ teaspoon ground nutmeg
½ of a 4-ounce container frozen whipped dessert topping, thawed

In a medium saucepan combine water and butter or margarine. Bring to boiling, stirring till butter melts. Add flour all at once, stirring vigorously. Cook and stir till mixture forms a ball that doesn't separate (see photo 1, page 98). Remove from heat and cool 10 minutes.

Add eggs, 1 at a time, beating with a wooden spoon after each addition till smooth (see photo 2, page 98). Drop batter by spoonfuls into 15 mounds, 3 inches apart, onto a greased baking sheet (see photo 3, page 99). Bake in a 400° oven for 25 to 30 minutes or till golden brown and puffy. Remove from oven. Cut off tops and remove any soft dough inside (see photo 4, page 99). Cool on a wire rack.

For filling, in a mixing bowl stir together pumpkin, sugar, ginger, and nutmeg. Fold thawed topping into mixture. To serve, spoon pumpkin filling into bottoms of cream puffs (see photo 5, page 99). Add cream puff tops. Makes 5 servings (3 filled cream puffs per serving).

Apricot Cream Puffs

6 Cream Puffs
⅓ cup sugar
1 tablespoon cornstarch
1¼ cups milk
1 beaten egg
1 tablespoon butter *or* margarine
½ cup dairy sour cream
Few drops almond extract
1 8¾-ounce can unpeeled apricot halves
2 tablespoons chopped pecans
Powdered sugar (optional)

Prepare Cream Puffs (see photos 1–4, page 98–99). For filling, in a small saucepan combine sugar and cornstarch. Stir in the milk (see photo 1, page 50). Cook and stir over medium heat till thickened and bubbly. Reduce heat, then cook and stir 2 minutes more. Remove from heat. Gradually stir about *half* the hot mixture into egg (see photo 2, page 50).

Return mixture to saucepan. Cook and stir till nearly bubbly (see photo 3, page 51). Reduce heat. Cook and stir 2 minutes more. Do not boil. Remove from heat. Stir in butter or margarine till melted. Stir in the sour cream and almond extract. Mix well.

Drain and cut up apricots. Fold apricots and pecans into filling mixture. Pour into a bowl. Cover surface with clear plastic wrap or waxed paper (see photo 4, page 51). Chill in refrigerator without stirring.

To serve, spoon apricot filling into bottoms of cream puffs (see photo 5, page 99). Add cream puff tops. If desired, sift powdered sugar lightly over tops of puffs. Makes 6 servings.

Cookies and Cream Puffs

Celebrate an everyday occasion with this scrumptious cookie-filled cream puff.

5   **Cream Puffs (see recipe, page 98)**
1   **cup whipping cream**
2   **tablespoons sugar**
1   **teaspoon vanilla**
1   **cup coarsely crushed chocolate sandwich cookies (8 cookies)**
     Powdered sugar (optional)

Prepare Cream Puffs (see photos 1–4, pages 98–99). For filling, in a small mixer bowl beat whipping cream, sugar, and vanilla till soft peaks form (tips curl). Fold in the cookies.

Spoon filling into bottoms of cream puffs (see photo 5, page 99). Add cream puff tops. Chill 1 hour before serving. If desired, sift powdered sugar lightly over tops of puffs. Serves 5.

Cannoli-Style Éclairs

These light éclairs are fashioned after Italian cannoli, a sweet ricotta-filled pastry.

12   **Éclairs (see recipe, below)**
1½   **cups ricotta cheese**
½   **cup sugar**
⅔   **cup miniature semisweet chocolate pieces**
¼   **cup chopped candied cherries**
½   **teaspoon vanilla**
1   **cup whipping cream**
2   **tablespoons shortening**
1   **teaspoon light corn syrup**
     Chopped pistachio nuts

Prepare Éclairs. For filling, in a mixing bowl stir together cheese and sugar. Stir in *⅓ cup* of the chocolate pieces, the cherries, and vanilla. Cover and chill filling.

Up to 1 hour before serving, beat whipping cream till soft peaks form (tips curl). Fold into ricotta mixture. Fill éclairs with ricotta filling. Melt remaining chocolate pieces, shortening, and corn syrup over low heat. Drizzle over éclairs and sprinkle with nuts. Chill. Makes 12 éclairs.

Making Éclairs

Prepare dough as for Cream Puffs (see recipe, page 98). Spoon some of the dough into a pastry tube fitted with a Number 10 or larger tip (½ to 1 inch in diameter).

Slowly pipe strips of dough onto a greased baking sheet, making each éclair about 4½ inches long, 1 inch wide, and ¾ inch high. Bake in a 400° oven for 35 to 40 minutes or till golden brown and puffy.

Remove from oven. Cut off the tops and remove any soft dough inside (see photo 4, page 99). Cool on a wire rack. Makes 12.

Flaky Phyllo Diamonds

Ever hear of a dessert that's built right in the pan? Here's one that is.

Start constructing this dessert masterpiece with layers of paper-thin phyllo dough, spreading each with melted butter. Then, stack with a mixture of nuts, coconut, sugar, and spices.

All these steps build up to the tastiest, flakiest, dessert you've ever put together.

Pecan-Coconut Baklava

Pecan-Coconut Baklava

Leftover diamond-shaped pieces make a great treat for later. Just wrap any extras and freeze them.

1	**16-ounce package frozen phyllo dough (18x14-inch rectangles)**
1½	**cups finely chopped pecans (about 6 ounces)**
1	**cup coconut**
¼	**cup packed brown sugar**
1	**teaspoon ground cinnamon**
¼	**teaspoon ground nutmeg**
1	**cup butter *or* margarine, melted**
¾	**cup sugar**
¾	**cup water**
2	**tablespoons honey**
2	**teaspoons lemon juice**

Thaw phyllo at room temperature or overnight in the refrigerator. Cut sheets in half crosswise. Cover with a damp towel (see photo 1). Butter the bottom of a 13x9x2-inch baking pan.

In a mixing bowl combine pecans, coconut, brown sugar, cinnamon, and nutmeg. Set aside. Layer *15 half-sheets* of phyllo in the pan, brushing *one-third* of melted butter or margarine between sheets (see photo 2). (Remove 1 sheet of phyllo at a time and keep remaining covered.)

Sprinkle *half* of nut mixture over phyllo in pan. Repeat with another *15 half-sheets* of phyllo, another third of butter or margarine, and remaining nut mixture. Top with remaining half-sheets of phyllo, brushing each one with some of the remaining third of butter.

Score top of phyllo into diamonds, making cuts about ¼ inch deep (see photo 3). Bake in a 350° oven for 40 to 45 minutes or till pastry is a deep golden brown.

Meanwhile, in a small saucepan combine sugar, water, and honey. Bring to boiling. Boil gently, uncovered, for 10 minutes. Remove from heat. Stir in lemon juice. Pour hot syrup over warm pastry (see photo 4). Cut into diamonds along the scored lines. Cool. Makes about 36 pieces.

1 Cut the stack of phyllo sheets in half, making 44 half-sheets that measure about 14x9 inches. Cover the phyllo with a damp towel to keep the dough from drying out, as shown. If the sheets dry out, they'll crumble as you work with them.

2 A soft pastry brush (about 1 inch wide) is a handy tool to use for spreading the melted butter or margarine over each phyllo sheet, as shown. *An important reminder:* Always cover the stack of phyllo dough with a damp towel after you remove each phyllo sheet.

3 To mark the top for scoring into diamonds, measure every 2½ inches along the long side of pan and mark with toothpicks. Measure every 1¾ inches along the short side of pan and mark.

Use a sharp knife and a ruler to score the top of the phyllo. The ruler helps you make straight, diagonal cuts from pick to pick, as shown. Make the cuts ¼ inch deep.

4 Boil sugar, water, and honey together, uncovered, to concentrate the syrup. After stirring in lemon juice, pour syrup as evenly as possible over baked pastry, as shown.

Magnificent Baked Soufflés

Wow your guests with a delicately light soufflé! Serve your beautiful soufflé right from the oven while it's standing tall.

Add to this culinary experience by making a big production out of the presentation of the dessert. As the soufflé finishes its last minutes in the oven, have guests ready in anticipation.

Brownie Soufflé

Brownie Soufflé

1 **6-ounce package (1 cup) semisweet chocolate pieces**
3 **tablespoons butter *or* margarine**
¼ **cup all-purpose flour**
⅛ **teaspoon salt**
¾ **cup milk**
4 **egg yolks**
4 **egg whites**
1 **teaspoon vanilla**
⅓ **cup sugar**
½ **cup whipping cream**
2 **tablespoons sifted powdered sugar**
   Chopped pecans

Attach a collar to an ungreased 1½-quart soufflé dish (see photo 1). Set aside. In a heavy saucepan over low heat stir chocolate pieces till chocolate begins to melt. Remove from heat. Stir till smooth. Set aside to cool.

In a small saucepan melt butter or margarine. Stir in flour and salt. Add milk. Cook and stir till very thick. Remove from heat. In a small mixer bowl beat egg yolks with an electric mixer on high speed about 5 minutes or till thick and lemon-colored. Gradually beat hot mixture into yolks (see photo 2). Stir in chocolate.

Wash the beaters. In a large mixer bowl beat egg whites and vanilla till soft peaks form (tips curl) (see photo 2, page 62). Gradually add sugar, beating on high speed till stiff peaks form (tips stand straight) (see photo 1, page 56). Fold a small amount of beaten egg whites into chocolate mixture to lighten it (see photo 3).

Then fold chocolate mixture into remaining beaten egg whites (see photo 4, page 57). Turn mixture into the prepared soufflé dish. Bake in a 325° oven for 55 to 60 minutes or till the soufflé is done (see photo 4).

Meanwhile, beat together whipping cream and powdered sugar till soft peaks form (see photo 2, page 44). Serve the soufflé at once. Pass whipped cream and nuts. Makes 6 servings.

1 Put a collar on a soufflé dish so that the soufflé can rise above the top of the dish without going over.

To make the collar, measure the circumference of the top of the dish and add 6 inches. Fold 12-inch-wide foil lengthwise into thirds. Lightly butter and sugar one side of foil (except 3 inches on each end). Attach foil, sugared side in, around the outside of the dish so that the foil extends about 2 inches above the dish. Make a series of locked folds until foil fits dish.

2 Slowly add the thickened mixture from the saucepan to the beaten egg yolks in the mixer bowl. Adding slowly helps prevent the hot mixture from cooking the egg yolks.

3 To make the thick chocolate mixture easier to work with, fold in a small portion of the fluffy egg white mixture.

4 To test for doneness, pull out the oven rack and insert a knife near the center. The knife should come out clean, as shown. When inserting the knife, enlarge the hole slightly so the crust doesn't clean the knife as it is pulled out.

Soufflé Café

3 tablespoons butter *or* margarine
¼ cup all-purpose flour
¼ cup sugar
1 teaspoon instant coffee crystals
⅔ cup milk
4 egg yolks
2 tablespoons coffee liqueur
4 egg whites
¼ cup sugar
½ cup whipping cream
1 tablespoon coffee liqueur

Attach collar to an ungreased 2-quart soufflé dish (see photo 1, page 108). Set the dish aside.

In a small saucepan melt butter or margarine. Stir in flour, ¼ cup sugar, and coffee crystals. Add milk. Cook and stir till mixture is thickened and bubbly, then cook and stir 1 minute more. Remove from heat.

In a small mixer bowl beat egg yolks with an electric mixer on high speed about 5 minutes or till thick and lemon-colored. Gradually beat the hot thickened mixture into beaten yolks (see photo 2, page 108). Beat in the 2 tablespoons coffee liqueur.

Wash the beaters thoroughly. In a large mixer bowl beat egg whites till soft peaks form (tips curl) (see photo 2, page 62). Gradually add ¼ cup sugar, beating on high speed till stiff peaks form (tips stand straight) (see photo 1, page 56). Fold egg yolk mixture into beaten egg whites (see photo 4, page 57). Turn mixture into the prepared soufflé dish. Bake in a 325° oven about 50 minutes or till a knife inserted near the center comes out clean (see photo 4, page 109).

Meanwhile, beat together whipping cream and 1 tablespoon liqueur till soft peaks form (tips curl). Serve soufflé immediately with whipped cream. Makes 8 servings.

Toasted Almond Soufflé

2 oranges
2 tablespoons butter *or* margarine
3 tablespoons all-purpose flour
½ cup skim milk
3 egg yolks
2 tablespoons finely chopped, toasted almonds
3 egg whites
3 tablespoons sugar
Strawberry-Orange Sauce

Attach collar to ungreased 1½-quart soufflé dish (see photo 1, page 108). Set aside. Finely shred enough orange peel to measure 1 teaspoon. Squeeze juice from oranges to measure 2 tablespoons for soufflé and ⅓ cup for Strawberry-Orange Sauce.

In a small saucepan melt butter. Stir in flour. Add milk. Cook and stir till thickened and bubbly, then cook and stir 1 minute more. Remove from heat. Stir in peel and 2 tablespoons juice. In a small mixer bowl beat yolks with an electric mixer on high speed 5 minutes. Gradually beat thickened mixture into beaten yolks (see photo 2, page 108). Stir in almonds.

Wash the beaters. In a large mixer bowl beat egg whites till soft peaks form (tips curl) (see photo 2, page 62). Gradually add sugar, beating till stiff peaks form (tips stand straight) (see photo 1, page 56). Fold orange-almond mixture into beaten egg whites (see photo 4, page 57). Turn into the prepared soufflé dish. Bake in a 325° oven for 40 to 45 minutes (see photo 4, page 109). Meanwhile, prepare Strawberry-Orange Sauce. Serve at once with sauce. Serves 6.

Strawberry-Orange Sauce: Slice 1 cup fresh *strawberries*. In a medium saucepan combine 2 tablespoons *sugar* and 1 teaspoon *cornstarch*. Stir in reserved ⅓ cup *orange juice*. Cook and stir till bubbly, then cook and stir 2 minutes more. Remove from heat. Cover surface with clear plastic wrap. Let stand till serving time. Stir sliced berries into cooled mixture. Makes 1 cup sauce.

Cheese Dessert Soufflé

A soufflé that tastes like a light cheesecake.

2 tablespoons butter *or* margarine
2 tablespoons all-purpose flour
Dash salt
⅔ cup milk
1 3-ounce package cream cheese, softened and cut up
¼ teaspoon finely shredded lemon peel
1 teaspoon lemon juice
3 egg yolks
3 egg whites
½ teaspoon vanilla
¼ cup sugar
Desired fresh fruit (sliced strawberries, pineapple tidbits, blueberries, dark sweet cherries, *or* sliced peaches)

Attach collar to an ungreased 1½-quart soufflé dish (see photo 1, page 108). Set dish aside.

In a small saucepan melt butter or margarine. Stir in flour and salt. Add milk. Cook and stir till mixture is thickened and bubbly, then cook and stir for 1 minute more. Turn heat to low. Add cheese, lemon peel, and lemon juice. Stir till cheese melts. Remove from heat.

In a small mixer bowl beat egg yolks with an electric mixer on high speed about 5 minutes or till thick and lemon-colored. Gradually beat hot thickened mixture into beaten yolks (see photo 2, page 108).

Wash the beaters thoroughly. In a large mixer bowl beat egg whites and vanilla till soft peaks form (tips curl) (see photo 2, page 62). Gradually add sugar, beating on high speed till stiff peaks form (tips stand straight) (see photo 1, page 56). Fold cheese mixture into beaten egg whites (see photo 4, page 57). Turn mixture into the prepared dish.

Bake in a 325° oven for 45 to 50 minutes or till a knife inserted near the center comes out clean (see photo 4, page 109). Remove collar. Serve immediately with fresh fruit. Serves 4 to 6.

Amaretto Bread Pudding Soufflé

½ cup milk
¼ cup sugar
¼ cup Amaretto
1½ cups dry bread cubes (about 2 slices of bread)
3 tablespoons butter *or* margarine
¼ cup all-purpose flour
⅛ teaspoon salt
¾ cup milk
4 egg yolks
4 egg whites
1 teaspoon vanilla
¼ cup sugar

Attach collar to an ungreased 2-quart soufflé dish (see photo 1, page 108). Set dish aside.

Combine ½ cup milk, ¼ cup sugar, and the Amaretto. Stir in bread cubes. Set mixture aside.

In a small saucepan melt butter or margarine. Stir in flour and salt. Add ¾ cup milk. Cook and stir till mixture is thickened and bubbly, then cook and stir for 1 minute more. Remove the saucepan from heat.

In a small mixer bowl beat egg yolks with an electric mixer on high speed about 5 minutes or till thick and lemon-colored. Gradually beat hot thickened mixture into beaten yolks (see photo 2, page 108). Stir in bread mixture.

Wash the beaters thoroughly. In a large mixer bowl beat egg whites and vanilla till soft peaks form (tips curl) (see photo 2, page 62). Gradually add ¼ cup sugar, beating on high speed till stiff peaks form (tips stand straight) (see photo 1, page 56). Fold bread mixture into beaten egg whites (see photo 4, page 57). Turn mixture into the prepared soufflé dish.

For a top hat on the soufflé, use a knife to trace a circle through the mixture about 1 inch from the edge. Bake in a 325° oven for 55 to 60 minutes or till a knife inserted near the center comes out clean (see photo 4, page 109). Serve immediately. Makes 6 servings.

Show-Off Gelatin Desserts

Make them now, serve them later! That's the key to these dressy desserts.

Get most of the fixing out of the way ahead of time. Then store the dessert in the refrigerator. All that's left are a few, if any, finishing touches at serving time.

Sound like an easy way to make a classy final course? It is. Give it a try and impress your family and friends!

Chilly Ribbon Soufflé

Chilly Ribbon Soufflé

1	cup loose-pack frozen red raspberries, thawed
7	tablespoons sugar
1	envelope unflavored gelatin
1¼	cups milk
4	slightly beaten egg yolks
1	teaspoon vanilla
4	egg whites
1	cup whipping cream
¼	cup chocolate-flavored syrup
¼	cup finely chopped almonds, toasted, *or* pistachios
	Few drops green food coloring (optional)
	Candy Leaves (optional)

Press raspberries through a sieve. Set raspberries aside; discard seeds. In a saucepan combine *4 tablespoons* of sugar and gelatin. Stir in milk and egg yolks. Cook and stir over medium heat till gelatin dissolves (see photo 1). Remove from heat. Stir in vanilla. Pour into a large mixing bowl. Chill till the mixture is the consistency of corn syrup, stirring occasionally (see photo 2). Remove from the refrigerator.

In a small mixer bowl immediately beat egg whites till soft peaks form (tips curl) (see photo 2, page 62). Gradually add *2 tablespoons* sugar, beating till stiff peaks form (tips stand straight) (see photo 1, page 56). When gelatin mixture is partially set (the consistency of unbeaten egg whites), fold in stiff-beaten egg whites (see photo 3). Beat *½ cup* of whipping cream till soft peaks form (see photo 2, page 44). Fold into gelatin mixture. Divide gelatin mixture into thirds (about 1¾ cups in each portion).

To *one third,* fold in chocolate. Transfer to a 1½-quart glass dish. Chill (see photo 4). Keep remaining gelatin at room temperature.

Fold almonds and food coloring, if desired, into second portion. Spoon atop chocolate mixture. Chill till nearly firm. Fold berries into remaining gelatin. Spoon over nut layer. Chill for 6 to 24 hours. To serve, beat remaining cream with remaining sugar. Pipe atop (see photo 5). If desired, trim with Candy Leaves. Serves 8.

Candy Leaves: Melt some colored confectioners' coating according to package directions. Use a small brush to paint the coating on the bottom of clean mint leaves. Place on plate and let harden so the leaf has a slight curve. Brush on a second layer. Harden. Peel off the leaf. Use Candy Leaves as a garnish.

1 Cook and stir the mixture till it is smooth-looking and free of any visible gelatin granules. If the mixture contains undissolved gelatin granules as shown on the left spoon, continue heating until the gelatin has dissolved, as shown on the right spoon. If the gelatin isn't completely dissolved, the dessert won't set up to a firm consistency.

5 To garnish the top, pipe whipped cream through a pastry bag using a large star tip. If desired, arrange the Candy Leaves in the whipped cream topping.

2 Remove the gelatin mixture from the refrigerator when it's the consistency of corn syrup, as shown. Even after it's taken from the refrigerator, the mixture continues to set up as it stands because it's so cold. Remove mixture from the refrigerator at this stage to slow the gelling down while you beat the egg whites and whipping cream.

3 The gelatin mixture is partially set when it's the consistency of unbeaten egg whites, as shown. Next, fold in other ingredients. Chill so that added ingredients stay evenly distributed throughout.

4 Before spooning on the next layer, lightly touch the gelatin to see if it's at the nearly firm stage. It should appear to be set but should feel sticky to the touch. Be careful not to chill the gelatin till completely firm or the layers may not hold together.

White Bavarian Soufflé

A glorious dessert that's destined to become a favorite.

2 tablespoons sugar
1 envelope unflavored gelatin
1¼ cups milk
4 ounces white confectioners' coating, cut up
4 slightly beaten egg yolks
¼ cup white créme de cacao
4 egg whites
2 tablespoons sugar
1 cup whipping cream
Toasted almonds *or* fresh fruit (optional)

In a saucepan combine 2 tablespoons sugar and gelatin. Stir in milk, confectioners' coating, and egg yolks. Cook and stir over medium heat till mixture thickens slightly and sugar and gelatin are dissolved (see photo 1, page 114). Remove gelatin mixture from heat.

Stir in crème de cacao. Chill in the refrigerator for 1½ to 2 hours or till mixture is the consistency of corn syrup, stirring occasionally (see photo 2, page 115). Remove from refrigerator.

In a small mixer bowl immediately beat egg whites till soft peaks form (tips curl) (see photo 2, page 62). Gradually add 2 tablespoons sugar, beating till stiff peaks form (tips stand straight) (see photo 1, page 56). When gelatin mixture is partially set (the consistency of unbeaten egg whites), fold in stiff-beaten egg whites (see photo 3, page 115). Whip cream till soft peaks form (see photo 2, page 44). Fold whipped cream into gelatin mixture.

Chill till mixture mounds when spooned. Transfer mixture to a 1½-quart soufflé or serving dish. Chill in the refrigerator 4 hours or till firm. To serve, garnish with toasted almonds or fresh fruit, if desired. Makes 6 servings.

Peach Bavarian

¼ cup sugar
1 envelope unflavored gelatin
½ cup cold water
1 cup frozen unsweetened peach slices, thawed
1 8-ounce carton peach yogurt
2 egg whites
2 tablespoons sugar
½ cup whipping cream

In a small saucepan combine ¼ cup sugar and gelatin. Stir in water. Cook and stir over medium heat till sugar and gelatin are dissolved (see photo 1, page 114). Remove gelatin mixture from heat.

In a blender container or food processor bowl place peach slices. Cover and blend or process till peaches are nearly smooth.

Stir puree into gelatin mixture. Gradually stir gelatin mixture into yogurt till combined. Chill in the refrigerator about 40 minutes or till the mixture is the consistency of corn syrup, stirring occasionally (see photo 2, page 115). Remove from the refrigerator.

In a small mixer bowl immediately beat egg whites till soft peaks form (tips curl) (see photo 2, page 62). Gradually add 2 tablespoons sugar, beating till stiff peaks form (tips stand straight) (see photo 1, page 56). Whip cream till soft peaks form (see photo 2, page 44).

When gelatin mixture is partially set (the consistency of unbeaten egg whites), fold in stiff-beaten egg whites and whipped cream (see photo 3, page 115). Chill about 20 minutes or till mixture mounds when spooned. Pile mixture into 8 dessert dishes and chill in the refrigerator 4 hours or till firm. Makes 8 servings.

Coconut Chiffon Dessert

½ **cup all-purpose flour**
2 **tablespoons brown sugar**
3 **tablespoons butter** *or* **margarine, melted**
1 **small fresh coconut**
Milk
⅓ **cup sugar**
1 **envelope unflavored gelatin**
2 **slightly beaten egg yolks**
1 **teaspoon vanilla**
2 **egg whites**
¼ **cup sugar**
½ **cup whipping cream**

For crumb mixture, in an 8x8x2-inch baking dish combine flour and brown sugar. Stir in butter or margarine. Spread in dish. Bake in a 350° oven for 15 minutes, stirring occasionally. Cool. Break up any large chunks. Set aside.

Pierce coconut eyes. Drain, reserving liquid. Add milk to liquid to measure *1⅓ cups*. Remove coconut shell, then remove brown skin. Coarsely shred enough coconut to make *2½ cups*. Spread *1½ cups* coconut in a shallow baking pan. Toast in 350° oven 15 to 20 minutes; stir occasionally. In a blender container or food processor bowl combine milk mixture and the 1 cup untoasted coconut. Blend smooth.

In a saucepan combine ⅓ cup sugar and gelatin. Stir in coconut liquid mixture and egg yolks. Cook and stir over medium heat till mixture thickens slightly and sugar and gelatin are dissolved (see photo 1, page 114). Remove the gelatin mixture from heat. Stir in vanilla. Transfer to a large bowl. Chill in the refrigerator for 1 to 1½ hours or till the mixture is the consistency of corn syrup, stirring occasionally (see photo 2, page 115). Remove from the refrigerator.

In a small mixer bowl beat egg whites till soft peaks form (see photo 2, page 62). Gradually add ¼ cup sugar, beating till stiff peaks form (tips stand straight) (see photo 1, page 56). When gelatin mixture is partially set (the consistency of unbeaten egg whites), fold in stiff-beaten egg whites (see photo 3, page 115).

Whip cream till soft peaks form (see photo 2, page 44). Set aside ½ cup of toasted coconut. Fold remaining toasted coconut and whipped cream into gelatin mixture. Place about ¼ cup of mixture in 8 parfait glasses. Top each with *1 rounded tablespoon* of crumb mixture. Divide remaining coconut mixture among the parfait glasses. Top each with *1 tablespoon* of reserved toasted coconut. Chill in the refrigerator 2 to 3 hours. Makes 8 servings.

Chocolate-Almond Mousse

It's unbeatable! Smooth, rich, and oh, so chocolaty.

2 **tablespoons sugar**
1 **teaspoon unflavored gelatin**
¾ **cup light cream** *or* **milk**
½ **of a 6-ounce package (½ cup) semisweet chocolate pieces**
Several dashes almond extract
½ **cup whipping cream**
2 **tablespoons sliced almonds, toasted**

In a small saucepan combine sugar and gelatin. Stir in light cream or milk and chocolate. Cook and stir over medium-low heat till bubbly and sugar and gelatin are dissolved and chocolate is melted (see photo 1, page 114). Remove from heat. Stir in extract. Chill in the refrigerator about 1 hour or till the mixture is the consistency of corn syrup, stirring occasionally (see photo 2, page 115). Remove from refrigerator.

Whip cream till soft peaks form (tips curl) (see photo 2, page 44). When gelatin mixture is partially set (the consistency of unbeaten egg whites), fold in whipped cream (see photo 3, page 115). Spoon into 4 dessert dishes. Chill in the refrigerator about 3 hours or till firm. To serve, sprinkle nuts atop. Makes 4 servings.

Daiquiri Torte

1¼ **cups sugar**
2 **envelopes unflavored gelatin**
1½ **cups water**
½ **cup lime juice**
3 **beaten egg yolks**
¼ **cup light rum**
2 **tablespoons orange liqueur**
12 **ladyfingers, split**
3 **egg whites**
¼ **cup sugar**
1 **cup whipping cream, whipped**

For filling, in a medium saucepan combine 1¼ cups sugar and gelatin. Stir in *¾ cup* of water, lime juice, and egg yolks. Cook and stir over medium heat till mixture just comes to a boil and gelatin dissolves (see photo 1, page 114). Remove from heat. Stir in remaining ¾ cup water, rum, and orange liqueur. Transfer to a bowl. Chill in the refrigerator about 1 hour or till the mixture is the consistency of corn syrup, stirring occasionally (see photo 2, page 115). Remove from refrigerator.

Meanwhile, line the bottom and sides of a 2½-quart mold or soufflé dish with waxed paper. Line the sides with split ladyfingers. Arrange 6 split ladyfingers in a spokelike fashion in bottom of mold, trimming to fit. Set aside.

In a small mixer bowl immediately beat egg whites till soft peaks form (tips curl) (see photo 2, page 62). Gradually add ¼ cup sugar, beating till stiff peaks form (tips stand straight) (see photo 1, page 56). When gelatin mixture is partially set (the consistency of unbeaten egg whites), fold in stiff-beaten egg whites and whipped cream (see photo 3, page 115). Spoon into the lined mold. Chill for 3 to 24 hours or till firm. To serve, unmold onto platter. Garnish with a few lime slices and mint leaves, if desired. Makes 12 servings.

◀ *Pictured opposite: Orange Bavarian Torte.*

Orange Bavarian Torte

½ **of a 17¼-ounce package (1 sheet) frozen puff pastry**
¾ **cup sugar**
1 **envelope unflavored gelatin**
¾ **cup milk**
2 **teaspoons finely shredded orange peel**
½ **cup orange juice**
3 **slightly beaten egg yolks**
3 **egg whites**
1 **cup whipping cream**

Thaw pastry according to package directions. On a lightly floured surface roll into a 12-inch square (see photo 1, page 88). Cut into a 12-inch circle. Transfer to an ungreased baking sheet. Prick at 1-inch intervals, making definite holes. Bake in a 375° oven for 20 to 25 minutes. Cool. Wrap and chill till serving time.

In a saucepan combine *½ cup* sugar and gelatin. Stir in milk, peel, juice, and egg yolks. Cook and stir over medium heat till mixture thickens slightly and gelatin is dissolved (see photo 1, page 114). Remove from heat. Transfer to a mixing bowl. Chill 50 minutes or till mixture is consistency of corn syrup; stir occasionally (see photo 2, page 115). Remove from refrigerator.

In a small mixer bowl immediately beat egg whites till soft peaks form (see photo 2, page 62). Gradually add remaining ¼ cup sugar, beating till stiff peaks form (see photo 1, page 56). When gelatin mixture is partially set (the consistency of unbeaten egg whites), fold in stiff-beaten egg whites (see photo 3, page 115). Beat *½ cup* whipping cream till soft peaks form (see photo 2, page 44). Fold into gelatin mixture. Lightly oil an 8-inch springform pan or 8x1½-inch round cake pan. Pour into pan. Chill for 2 to 24 hours or till firm.

To serve, unmold gelatin mixture atop center of pastry circle so an edge of pastry shows around outside of filling. Beat remaining cream and pipe around pastry edge. Garnish with whipped cream, kiwi fruit half-slices, and halved strawberries, if desired. Makes 10 servings.

Dinner Finalés

When appetites are satisfied and it's time to sit back and relax, enjoy a light dinner finalé. Bring on a tray of steaming dessert coffees with a colorful arrangement of assorted fresh fruit and special cheeses. It's a simple yet sumptuous way to wrap up the evening.

Dessert coffees

Preparing a coffee special enough for dessert is simple. Just buy a flavored dessert coffee or dress up your everyday brew.

Check the selection of dessert coffees in a specialty coffee shop. You'll find a wide variety, ranging from flavored regular coffee to decaffeinated blends. Some coffees are flavored with spices, vanilla, or even chocolate.

Make your everyday brew special by stirring in a complementary liqueur. Coffee liqueur is an obvious choice. Others you might try include almond, apple brandy, chocolate, cherry, orange, or cream liqueurs. Use your imagination!

Then top them with pressurized whipped cream and ground cinnamon, nutmeg, or chocolate. Or, include a cinnamon stirring stick.

Fresh fruit

Now's the time to try some new or unusual fruits you've seen in your supermarket—kiwi fruit, papayas, mangoes,

pomegranates, for example. Then team them up with old favorites—strawberries, apples, grapes, pears. Pick what's in season.

Arrange a colorful assortment of cut and uncut fruit on a tray. Any combination will do. Choose your fruit according to colors that will brighten the tray.

Special cheeses

Complete your tray of fruit with a few cheeses. Remove the cheeses from the refrigerator about an hour before serving so they'll be at their best flavor.

Use the following list as a guide to choosing dessert cheeses. If you can, try to taste the cheese before you buy.
● *Bel Paese:* This soft cheese ranges from robust to delicately rich and sweet in flavor. Choose the sweet variety for dessert.
● *Brie:* A creamy, rich cheese that's both smooth and tangy in flavor. The thin, edible crust hides the creamy interior. The inside of this flavorful cheese can be firm, or if well-ripened, very soft.

● *Cream cheese:* Chocolate, strawberry, you name it—you'll find this mild and soft spreadable cheese in many flavors.
● *Camembert:* Another suitable dessert cheese with an edible white crust. It tastes slightly bitter and yeasty—a great match for fruit.
● *Edam:* You'll recognize this as the cheese that's shaped like a flattened ball and has a red paraffin coating. It's mild and nutty in flavor and firm in texture.
● *Gjetost:* A hard, solid cheese with caramellike color and flavor. Serve this cheese sliced thin.

● *Gouda:* Shaped like Edam, Gouda has a yellow-orange interior. It has a light, nutty flavor.
● *Gourmandise:* A soft, creamy cheese spread that's flavored with kirsch, a cherry brandy.
● *Gruyère:* This nutty, mild cheese is firm, with small holes.
● *Havarti:* Cream-colored Havarti's flavor varies from mild to strong. Choose the mild variety.
● *Jarlsberg:* Jarlsberg has small holes, like Swiss cheese, but a very mild flavor.
● *Port du Salut:* A buttery, delicately flavored cheese. It tastes zestier when aged.

Nutrition Analysis Chart

Use these analyses to compare nutritional values of different recipes. This information was calculated using Agriculture Handbook Number 8, published by the United States Department of Agriculture, as the primary source.

In compiling the nutrition analyses, we made the following assumptions:

- Garnishes and optional ingredients were not included in the nutrition analyses.
- When two ingredient options appear in a recipe, calculations were made using the first one.
- For ingredients of variable weight or for recipes with a serving range ("Makes 4 to 6 servings"), calculations were made using the first figure.

	Per Serving						Percent U.S. RDA Per Serving							
	Calories	Protein (g)	Carbohydrate (g)	Fat (g)	Sodium (mg)	Potassium (mg)	Protein	Vitamin A	Vitamin C	Thiamine	Riboflavin	Niacin	Calcium	Iron
Cheesecakes														
Apricot Cheesecake (p. 74)	337	7	35	20	178	186	10	34	7	7	11	4	5	8
Calorie-Trimmed Cheesecake (p. 79)	198	7	19	11	190	113	11	10	12	2	9	1	9	3
Cottage Cheese Cheesecake (p. 76)	380	9	29	27	341	176	13	20	12	3	15	3	8	7
Individual Pumpkin Cheesecakes (p. 76)	341	6	25	25	270	153	9	48	2	2	9	1	6	5
Poppy Seed Cheesecake (p. 77)	515	10	50	31	266	122	16	24	2	12	14	4	18	17
Triple Chocolate Cheesecake (p. 79)	483	8	41	34	260	187	13	22	0	4	13	3	7	11
Cookies and Cakes														
Banana-Orange Soft Drops (p. 16)	71	1	12	3	48	20	1	2	1	2	1	1	1	1
Carrot-Orange Bars (p. 19)	94	1	14	4	79	44	2	18	1	3	3	2	2	2
Chocolate Tunnel Peanut Cake (p. 32)	460	9	62	21	272	208	14	11	1	14	12	19	7	11
Cocoa Streusel Cake (p. 34)	372	4	52	18	217	112	7	4	0	10	7	7	2	11
Coconut-Oatmeal Cookies (p. 18)	72	1	8	4	35	28	1	1	0	2	1	1	1	2
Double-Chocolate Pudding Drops (p. 18)	86	1	11	5	48	32	2	0	0	2	2	1	2	3
Lemony Carrot Cake (p. 34)	305	4	49	11	322	111	6	49	3	9	7	5	4	7
Peanut Butter Drops (p. 18)	93	2	12	4	59	63	3	1	0	2	3	4	2	3
Spicy Date Drop Cookies (p. 19)	55	1	8	3	31	49	1	1	1	2	2	2	1	2
Streusel Cupcakes (p. 34)	140	2	19	7	82	42	3	1	0	4	3	2	1	4
Topsy-Turvy Spice Cake (p. 35)	358	4	53	16	231	304	5	12	1	11	9	7	9	15
Tropical-Topped Cake (p. 35)	395	5	59	17	215	166	7	3	3	13	8	8	8	13
Cream Puffs														
Apricot Cream Puffs (p. 100)	337	8	28	22	247	232	12	31	3	10	15	5	11	8
Cannoli-Style Eclairs (p. 101)	360	8	27	25	193	138	12	16	1	7	11	3	12	7
Cookies and Cream Puffs (p. 101)	420	6	27	33	270	85	9	23	0	9	11	5	5	7
Cream Puffs (p. 98)	159	4	10	12	175	41	6	9	0	6	7	3	2	5
Éclairs (p. 101)	132	3	8	10	146	34	5	8	0	5	6	3	1	5
Orange-Filled Cream Puffs (p. 98)	400	8	51	19	248	305	12	23	43	14	15	5	11	9
Slimming Pumpkin Puffs (p. 100)	189	4	21	10	128	85	6	47	1	6	8	4	3	7

	Per Serving					Percent U.S. RDA Per Serving							
	Calories	Protein (g)	Carbohydrate (g)	Fat (g)	Sodium (mg)	Potassium (mg)	Protein	Vitamin A	Vitamin C	Thiamine	Riboflavin	Niacin	Calcium	Iron

Crepes

	Calories	Protein (g)	Carbohydrate (g)	Fat (g)	Sodium (mg)	Potassium (mg)	Protein	Vitamin A	Vitamin C	Thiamine	Riboflavin	Niacin	Calcium	Iron
Apricot Crepes (p. 84)	325	11	46	12	166	323	16	37	7	10	16	7	20	8
Calorie Counter's Crepes (p. 82)	42	2	7	0	36	52	3	1	0	4	5	2	3	2
Calorie-Cutting Cantaloupe Crepes (p. 85)	200	7	28	5	99	379	10	48	48	11	13	6	12	6
Chocolate Coconut-Cream Crepes (p. 85)	311	7	42	14	139	226	10	6	12	9	15	5	12	7
Dessert Crepes (p. 82)	63	2	9	2	37	50	4	1	1	4	5	2	3	3
Nutty Crème Crepes (p. 84)	282	6	30	16	86	188	10	7	2	10	13	5	10	7
Strawberry-Pineapple Crepe Cup Flambé (p. 83)	155	3	31	3	38	208	4	2	53	7	8	3	5	5

Frozen Desserts

	Calories	Protein (g)	Carbohydrate (g)	Fat (g)	Sodium (mg)	Potassium (mg)	Protein	Vitamin A	Vitamin C	Thiamine	Riboflavin	Niacin	Calcium	Iron
Apple Pie Ice Cream (p. 41)	233	3	24	14	57	86	5	10	2	2	6	0	7	6
Apricot-Orange Sherbet (p. 59)	162	5	37	0	92	327	8	29	9	3	10	2	15	2
Banana-Pecan Ice Cream (p. 40)	231	3	20	16	45	184	5	11	3	4	9	1	9	2
Chocolate Chip Ice Cream (p. 38)	301	2	23	23	33	95	4	16	1	1	6	0	6	2
Chocolate Ice Cream (p. 38)	296	2	26	21	39	107	4	16	1	2	6	0	6	2
Easy Vanilla Ice Cream (p. 38)	266	2	19	21	33	72	3	16	1	1	6	0	6	1
Ginger-Raisin Ice Cream (p. 40)	226	3	19	16	77	144	5	12	1	3	7	1	7	3
Honey-Grapefruit Ice (p. 58)	103	0	28	0	2	88	1	0	27	1	1	1	1	1
Kiwi Fruit Sherbet (p. 59)	146	2	34	1	29	217	4	2	65	1	5	1	4	1
Lime Sherbet (p. 58)	163	5	31	3	56	192	7	2	11	3	10	1	14	0
Strawberry Ice Cream (p. 38)	277	2	22	21	33	84	3	16	9	2	6	0	6	1
Strawberry Sorbet (p. 56)	101	2	22	1	28	197	4	1	68	3	6	1	4	2

Fruit Desserts

	Calories	Protein (g)	Carbohydrate (g)	Fat (g)	Sodium (mg)	Potassium (mg)	Protein	Vitamin A	Vitamin C	Thiamine	Riboflavin	Niacin	Calcium	Iron
Apple-Granola Crisp (p. 13)	154	1	27	6	72	198	2	4	8	4	3	2	1	3
Blueberry Cobbler (p. 28)	295	4	50	10	246	165	5	8	13	13	9	8	9	9
Caramel Pear-Peach Crisp (p. 12)	411	6	65	16	203	425	9	17	13	10	16	6	12	8
Cherry-Berry Cobbler (p. 26)	288	4	54	7	245	216	6	8	8	8	7	5	7	7
Easy-as-Pie Cobbler (p. 29)	321	2	66	6	287	120	3	2	10	7	4	4	3	32
Elegant Baked Pears (p. 23)	205	1	42	3	1	243	2	1	8	3	6	2	3	4
Gingery Apricot-Banana Compote (p. 9)	151	1	35	2	7	395	2	25	35	4	3	4	2	6
Orange-Sauced Baked Apples (p. 22)	240	2	58	2	92	356	3	2	36	6	3	3	7	6
Peach-Granola Crisp (p. 13)	149	2	25	6	71	383	3	21	13	4	6	10	1	3
Pear-Cranberry Cobbler (p. 29)	364	4	62	13	248	227	6	7	30	9	8	6	12	9
Poached Nectarines and Grapes (p. 8)	134	1	34	1	1	284	2	16	15	3	3	6	1	2
Spicy Pineapple Cobbler (p. 28)	203	3	42	3	123	233	4	4	27	15	6	6	9	6

Gelatin Desserts

	Calories	Protein (g)	Carbohydrate (g)	Fat (g)	Sodium (mg)	Potassium (mg)	Protein	Vitamin A	Vitamin C	Thiamine	Riboflavin	Niacin	Calcium	Iron
Chocolate-Almond Mousse (p. 117)	316	4	21	26	25	150	7	13	1	1	7	1	6	4
Coconut Chiffon Dessert (p. 117)	388	6	31	28	92	237	10	10	2	6	10	3	7	8
Daiquiri Torte (p. 119)	250	4	36	10	31	50	6	9	5	3	6	1	3	3
Orange Bavarian Torte (p. 119)	235	4	23	15	95	89	7	10	10	2	7	1	5	2
Peach Bavarian (p. 116)	132	3	18	6	36	120	5	7	3	1	6	1	5	0

Meringues

	Calories	Protein (g)	Carbohydrate (g)	Fat (g)	Sodium (mg)	Potassium (mg)	Protein	Vitamin A	Vitamin C	Thiamine	Riboflavin	Niacin	Calcium	Iron
Double Chocolate Meringues (p. 64)	305	4	37	17	45	96	6	10	0	1	7	0	3	3
Individual Chocolate Meringue Shells (p. 62)	129	1	28	2	19	35	2	0	0	0	2	0	2	0

	Per Serving						Percent U.S. RDA Per Serving						
	Calories	Protein (g)	Carbohydrate (g)	Fat (g)	Sodium (mg)	Potassium (mg)	Protein	Vitamin A	Vitamin C	Thiamine	Riboflavin	Niacin	Calcium	Iron
Meringues *(continued)*														
Individual Meringue Shells (p. 62)	102	1	25	0	19	18	2	0	0	0	2	0	0	0
Meringue Shell (p. 62)	102	1	25	0	19	18	2	0	0	0	2	0	0	0
Nut Meringue Shell (p. 62)	152	3	27	4	19	82	4	0	0	1	6	2	2	2
Peach Meringue Tart (p. 65)	300	4	42	14	60	218	6	13	7	2	10	4	5	3
Sour Cream-Lemon Meringue Tart (p. 63)	237	4	35	10	45	103	5	8	7	2	8	0	7	2
Strawberry Torte (p. 64)	235	3	27	13	37	169	5	9	53	2	9	1	4	2
Pies and Pastries														
Apple-Berry Turnovers (p. 95)	262	3	37	12	92	76	5	1	5	12	7	8	1	7
Double-Crust Pastry (p. 92)	261	3	24	17	134	30	5	0	0	13	7	8	1	8
Coconut Tart (p. 88)	309	5	45	13	153	145	8	4	1	3	9	1	9	4
Ginger Peachy Pie (p. 93)	395	4	54	19	155	257	6	7	6	15	10	13	3	14
Java Cream Pie (p. 94)	436	7	48	26	124	196	10	8	2	11	15	6	10	8
Pecan-Coconut Baklava (p. 104)	304	2	32	20	390	96	4	8	1	12	4	6	2	6
Single-Crust Pastry (p. 92)	145	2	15	9	67	19	3	0	0	8	4	5	0	5
Summer Fruit Tart (p. 94)	366	4	41	21	178	176	7	8	25	14	10	8	4	7
Wrapped Pear Dumplings (p. 95)	574	5	78	28	228	224	8	7	9	19	12	11	3	14
Puddings and Custards														
Baked Cottage Cheese Custard (p. 70)	155	10	21	4	213	153	15	5	1	3	13	1	10	3
Cheesecake Pudding Parfaits (p. 53)	407	9	36	26	285	307	14	18	3	8	22	4	18	7
Chocolate Pudding (p. 52)	330	7	38	18	134	285	10	9	3	5	16	1	18	6
Citrus Pudding Parfaits (p. 50)	501	4	70	26	66	360	6	12	92	12	5	3	4	9
Hot Cocoa Pudding (p. 52)	277	7	43	10	171	236	11	7	3	7	16	3	16	7
Individual Custards (p. 68)	166	8	17	8	231	187	12	6	2	4	15	0	13	5
Liqueur-Flavored Pudding (p. 52)	246	6	32	11	134	216	9	9	3	5	15	0	18	3
Peachy Rice Pudding (p. 70)	237	8	39	6	136	264	12	13	5	7	15	4	13	7
Pumpkin Pudding (p. 53)	151	5	28	3	148	255	7	55	5	4	9	2	12	3
Rum-Sauced Custard Ring (p. 68)	210	8	25	8	168	246	12	6	2	5	16	1	15	8
Stirred Custard (p. 71)	23	1	2	1	13	25	2	1	0	1	2	0	2	1
Tangy Vanilla Pudding (p. 52)	217	5	19	14	91	201	8	11	3	4	14	1	16	2
Tropical Bread Pudding (p. 70)	332	11	39	16	203	289	16	6	4	11	21	6	16	11
Versatile Vanilla Pudding (p. 52)	223	6	26	11	134	216	9	9	3	5	15	1	18	3
Shortcakes														
Apple-Orange Shortcakes (p. 46)	540	6	53	35	361	312	9	19	56	19	14	10	16	9
Banana Split Shortcakes (p. 47)	366	4	52	17	210	249	6	13	73	12	12	8	12	9
Chocolate-Nectarine Shortcake (p. 44)	467	6	58	25	283	334	10	34	10	14	15	13	11	10
Easy Fruit-Yogurt Shortcake (p. 46)	379	8	52	16	554	260	12	5	1	12	17	5	30	9
Pear-Berry Nut Cake (p. 47)	484	7	66	23	282	295	11	14	11	20	18	10	17	11
Soufflés														
Amaretto Bread Pudding Soufflé (p. 111)	275	7	36	12	213	134	11	10	1	8	14	3	9	6
Brownie Soufflé (p. 108)	421	7	36	30	165	210	12	15	1	7	13	2	8	9
Cheese Dessert Soufflé (p. 111)	292	8	23	19	219	245	13	17	62	6	17	2	10	8
Chilly Ribbon Soufflé (p. 114)	290	7	29	18	66	203	11	13	10	4	13	2	10	6
Soufflé Café (p. 110)	222	4	21	13	89	82	7	11	1	4	9	1	5	4
Toasted Almond Soufflé (p. 110)	174	5	21	8	80	197	8	7	54	5	10	2	6	5
White Bavarian Soufflé (p. 116)	395	8	25	28	95	191	13	17	2	4	14	0	14	4

A-B

Amaretto Bread Pudding
  Soufflé, 111
Apples
  Apple-Berry Turnovers, 95
  Apple-Granola Crisp, 13
  Apple-Orange Shortcakes, 46
  Apple Pie Ice Cream, 41
  Easy-as-Pie Cobbler, 29
  Orange-Sauced Baked
    Apples, 22
Apricots
  Apricot Cheesecake, 74
  Apricot Cream Puffs, 100
  Apricot Crepes, 84
  Apricot-Orange Sherbet, 59
Baked Cottage Cheese
  Custard, 70
Baklava, Pecan-Coconut, 104
Bananas
  Banana-Orange Soft Drops, 16
  Banana-Pecan Ice Cream, 40
  Banana Split Shortcakes, 47
  Gingery Apricot-Banana
    Compote, 9
Berries
  Apple-Berry Turnovers, 95
  Blueberry Cobbler, 28
  Calorie-Trimmed
    Cheesecake, 79
  Strawberry Ice Cream, 38
  Strawberry-Pineapple Crepe
    Cup Flambé, 83
  Strawberry Sorbet, 56
  Strawberry Torte, 64
Brownie Soufflé, 108
Butter Frosting, 16

C

Cakes
  Apple-Orange Shortcakes, 46
  Banana Split Shortcakes, 47
  Chocolate-Nectarine
    Shortcake, 44
  Chocolate Tunnel Peanut
    Cake, 32
  Cocoa Streusel Cake, 34
  Easy Fruit-Yogurt
    Shortcake, 46
  Lemony Carrot Cake, 34
  Pear-Berry Nut Cake, 47
  Topsy-Turvy Spice Cake, 35
  Tropical-Topped Cake, 35
Calorie Counter's Crepes, 82
Calorie-Cutting Cantaloupe
  Crepes, 85
Calorie-Trimmed Cheesecake, 79
Cannoli-Style Éclairs, 101
Caramel Pear-Peach Crisp, 12
Carrot-Orange Bars, 19
Cheesecakes
  Apricot Cheesecake, 74
  Calorie-Trimmed
    Cheesecake, 79
  Cheese Dessert Soufflé, 111
  Cheesecake Pudding
    Parfaits, 53

Cheesecakes *(continued)*
  Cottage Cheese
    Cheesecake, 76
  Individual Pumpkin
    Cheesecakes, 76
  Poppy Seed Cheesecake, 77
  Triple Chocolate
    Cheesecake, 79
Cheese Dessert Soufflé, 111
Cherry-Berry Cobbler, 26
Chilly Ribbon Soufflé, 114
Chocolate
  Brownie Soufflé, 108
  Cannoli-Style Éclairs, 101
  Chocolate-Almond
    Mousse, 117
  Chocolate Chip Ice
    Cream, 38
  Chocolate Coconut-Cream
    Crepes, 85
  Chocolate Ice Cream, 38
  Chocolate-Nectarine
    Shortcake, 44
  Chocolate Pudding, 52
  Chocolate Tunnel Peanut
    Cake, 32
  Cocoa Streusel Cake, 34
  Cookies and Cream Puffs, 101
  Double Chocolate
    Meringues, 64
  Double-Chocolate Pudding
    Drops, 18
  Hot Cocoa Pudding, 52
  Individual Chocolate Meringue
    Shells, 62
  Java Cream Pie, 94
  Triple Chocolate
    Cheesecake, 79
Citrus Pudding Parfaits, 50

Cobblers
  Blueberry Cobbler, 28
  Cherry-Berry Cobbler, 26
  Easy-as-Pie Cobbler, 29
  Pear-Cranberry Cobbler, 29
  Spicy Pineapple Cobbler, 28
Cocoa Streusel Cake, 34
Coconut
  Coconut Chiffon Dessert, 117
  Coconut-Oatmeal Cookies, 18
  Coconut Tart, 88
Compotes
  Gingery Apricot-Banana
    Compote, 9
  Poached Nectarines and
    Grapes, 8
Cookies
  Banana-Orange Soft Drops, 16
  Carrot-Orange Bars, 19
  Coconut-Oatmeal Cookies, 18
  Cookies and Cream Puffs, 101
  Double-Chocolate Pudding
    Drops, 18
  Peanut Butter Drops, 18
  Spicy Date Drop Cookies, 19
Cooling a cake, 33
Coring fruit, 22
Cottage Cheese Cheesecake, 76
Cream Cheese Frosting, 19
Cream Puffs
  Apricot Cream Puffs, 100
  Cannoli-Style Éclairs, 101
  Cookies and Cream Puffs, 101
  Cream Puffs, 98
  Orange-Filled Cream Puffs, 98
  Slimming Pumpkin Puffs, 100

Crème Fraîche, 84
Crepes
  Apricot Crepes, 84
  Calorie Counter's
    Crepes, 82
  Calorie-Cutting Cantaloupe
    Crepes, 85
  Chocolate Coconut-Cream
    Crepes, 85
  Dessert Crepe Cups, 82
  Dessert Crepes, 82
  Nutty Crème Crepes, 84
  Nutty Dessert Crepes, 82
  Strawberry-Pineapple Crepe
    Cup Flambé, 83
Crisps
  Apple-Granola Crisp, 13
  Caramel Pear-Peach Crisp, 12
  Peach-Granola Crisp, 13

D-F

Daiquiri Torte, 119
Dessert Crepe Cups, 82
Dessert Crepes, 82
Double Chocolate Meringues, 64
Double-Chocolate Pudding
  Drops, 18
Double-Crust Pastry, 92
Easy-as-Pie Cobbler, 29
Easy Fruit-Yogurt Shortcake, 46
Easy Vanilla Ice Cream, 38

Elegant Baked Pears, 23
Fruits (*see also* Apples, Apricots
    Bananas, Berries, Peaches,
    Pears, and Strawberries)
  Calorie-Cutting Cantaloupe
    Crepes, 85
  Cheese Dessert Soufflé, 111
  Cherry-Berry Cobbler, 26
  Citrus Pudding Parfaits, 50
  Honey-Grapefruit Ice, 58
  Kiwi Fruit Sherbet, 59
  Lime Sherbet, 58
  Orange Bavarian Torte, 119
  Orange-Filled Cream Puffs, 98
  Poached Nectarines and
    Grapes, 8
  Sour Cream-Lemon Meringue
    Tart, 63
  Spicy Date Drop Cookies, 19
  Spicy Pineapple Cobbler, 28
  Summer Fruit Tart, 94
  Tropical-Topped Cake, 35
Fudge Sauce, 41

G-L

Gelatin Desserts
  Chilly Ribbon Soufflé, 114
  Chocolate-Almond
    Mousse, 117
  Coconut Chiffon Dessert, 117
  Daiquiri Torte, 119
  Orange Bavarian Torte, 119
  Peach Bavarian, 116
  White Bavarian Soufflé, 116
Ginger Peachy Pie, 93
Ginger-Raisin Ice Cream, 40

Gingery Apricot-Banana
  Compote, 9
Greasing and flouring a pan, 32
Honey-Grapefruit Ice, 58
Hot Cocoa Pudding, 52
How Do You Know Your
  Cheesecake Is Done?, 77
Ice Cream
  Apple Pie Ice Cream, 41
  Banana-Pecan Ice Cream, 40
  Chocolate Chip Ice Cream, 38
  Chocolate Ice Cream, 38
  Easy Vanilla Ice Cream, 38
  Ginger-Raisin Ice Cream, 40
  Strawberry Ice Cream, 38
Individual Chocolate Meringue
  Shells, 62
Individual Meringue Shells, 62
Individual Pumpkin
  Cheesecakes, 76
Java Cream Pie, 94
Kiwi Fruit Sherbet, 59
Lemon Frosting, 34
Lemony Carrot Cake, 34
Lime Sherbet, 58
Liqueur-Flavored Pudding, 52

M-O

Making a soufflé, 108
Making a syrup, 8
Making cream puffs, 98
Making crepes, 82
Making gelatin desserts, 114
Making pie pastry, 92
Marshmallow Topping, 41

Meringues
  Double Chocolate
    Meringues, 64
  Individual Chocolate Meringue
    Shells, 62
  Individual Meringue Shells, 62
  Meringue Shell, 62
  Nut Meringue Shell, 62
  Peach Meringue Tart, 65
  Pie-Top Meringues, 65
  Poached Meringues, 65
  Sour Cream-Lemon Meringue
    Tart, 63
  Strawberry Torte, 64
Nutty Crème Crepes, 84
Nutty Dessert Crepes, 82
Oranges
  Orange Bavarian Torte, 119
  Orange-Filled Cream Puffs, 98
  Orange-Sauced Baked
    Apples, 22

P

Peaches
  Ginger Peachy Pie, 93
  Peach Bavarian, 116
  Peach-Granola Crisp, 13
  Peach Meringue Tart, 65
  Peachy Rice Pudding, 70
Peanut Butter Drops, 18
Peanut Butter Glaze, 32
Pears
  Caramel Pear-Peach Crisp, 12
  Elegant Baked Pears, 23

Pears (continued)
  Pear-Berry Nut Cake, 47
  Pear-Cranberry Cobbler, 29
  Wrapped Pear Dumplings, 95
Pecan-Coconut Baklava, 104
Peeling and coring pears, 12
Pies
  Apple-Berry Turnovers, 95
  Coconut Tart, 88
  Double-Crust Pastry, 92
  Ginger Peachy Pie, 93
  Java Cream Pie, 94
  Single-Crust Pastry, 92
  Summer Fruit Tart, 94
  Wrapped Pear Dumplings, 95
Poppy Seed Cheesecake, 77
Praline Sauce, 41
Puddings and Custards
  Baked Cottage Cheese
    Custard, 70
  Cheesecake Pudding
    Parfaits, 53
  Chocolate Pudding, 52
  Citrus Pudding Parfaits, 50
  Hot Cocoa Pudding, 52
  Liqueur-Flavored Pudding, 52
  Peachy Rice Pudding, 70
  Pumpkin Pudding, 53
  Rum-Sauced Custard Ring, 68
  Stirred Custard, 71
  Tangy Vanilla Pudding, 52
  Tropical Bread Pudding, 70
  Versatile Vanilla Pudding, 52
Pumpkin
  Individual Pumpkin
    Cheesecakes, 76
  Pumpkin Pudding, 53
  Slimming Pumpkin Puffs, 100

R-Z

Removing peel from an
   orange 8,
Rum-Sauced Custard Ring, 68
Sherbets and Ices
   Apricot-Orange Sherbet, 59
   Honey-Grapefruit Ice, 58
   Kiwi Fruit Sherbet, 59
   Lime Sherbet, 58
   Strawberry Sorbet, 56
Single-Crust Pastry, 92
Slimming Pumpkin Puffs, 100
Soufflés
   Amaretto Bread Pudding
      Soufflé, 111
   Brownie Soufflé, 108
   Cheese Dessert Soufflé, 111
   Chilly Ribbon Soufflé, 114
   Soufflé Café, 110
   Toasted Almond Soufflé, 110
   White Bavarian Soufflé, 116
Sour Cream-Lemon Meringue
   Tart, 63
Spicy Date Drop Cookies, 19
Spicy Pineapple Cobbler, 28
Strawberries
   Strawberry Ice Cream, 38
   Strawberry-Orange Sauce, 110
   Strawberry-Pineapple Crepe
      Cup Flambé, 83
   Strawberry Sorbet, 56
   Strawberry Torte, 64

Streusel Cupcakes, 34
Summer Fruit Tart, 94
Tangy Vanilla Pudding, 52
Toasted Almond Soufflé, 110
Topsy-Turvy Spice Cake, 35
Triple Chocolate Cheesecake, 79
Tropical Bread Pudding, 70
Tropical-Topped Cake, 35
Using an ice cream freezer, 38
Versatile Vanilla Pudding, 52
White Bavarian Soufflé, 116
Wrapped Pear Dumplings, 95

Tips

Attention, Microwave
   Owners!, 29
Crepe Shaping, 85
Dinner Finalés, 120
Ice Cream Toppers, 41
Individual Custards, 68
Making Eclairs, 101
Ripening, 40
So-Soft Meringues, 65
Stirred Custard, 71